The 'Local' Irish in the West of Scotland

DOI: 10.1057/9781137329844

Also by Geraldine Vaughan

Le Monde britannique 1815–1931 (with C. Berthezène, P. Purseigle, J. Vincent, 2010)

DOI: 10.1057/9781137329844

palgrave▸pivot

The 'Local' Irish in the West of Scotland, 1851–1921

Geraldine Vaughan

DOI: 10.1057/9781137329844

© Geraldine Vaughan 2013

First published 2013 by
PALGRAVE MACMILLAN

Palgrave Macmillan in the UK is an imprint of Macmillan Publishers Limited, registered in England, company number 785998, of Houndmills, Basingstoke, Hampshire RG21 6XS.

Palgrave Macmillan in the US is a division of St Martin's Press LLC, 175 Fifth Avenue, New York, NY 10010.

Palgrave Macmillan is the global academic imprint of the above companies and has companies and representatives throughout the world.

Palgrave® and Macmillan® are registered trademarks in the United States, the United Kingdom, Europe and other countries.

ISBN: 978–1–137–32985–1 EPUB
ISBN: 978–1–137–32984–4 PDF
ISBN: 978–1–137–32983–7 Hardback

A catalogue record for this book is available from the British Library.

A catalog record for this book is available from the Library of Congress.

www.palgrave.com/pivot

DOI: 10.1057/9781137329844

▶ *In loving memory of Major Michael Vincent Vaughan (†2001),*
Lishy Harkins (†2006) & Brendan Harkins (†2011)

DOI: 10.1057/9781137329844

Contents

DOI: 10.1057/9781137329844

DOI: 10.1057/9781137329844

List of Tables

DOI: 10.1057/9781137329844

List of Figures

Acknowledgments

I wish to place on record my thanks to the staff of the Scottish Catholic Archives who allowed me the use of the transcript of a Greenock Elector poster (Michael Condon papers) [Appendix 2].

I am very grateful to the staff of the Airdrie Library (Local History Room), especially Monica Ferguson and Marion; to Mary McHugh at the Glasgow Archdiocese Archives; to the staff of the Scottish Catholic Archives and the National Archives of Scotland in Edinburgh and to the staff of the North Lanarkshire Archives and the Glasgow City Archives. The Rouen Genealogy Centre allowed me to work on Scottish census enumeration rolls, and thus spared me extra travelling time. I am also indebted to the Association Franco-Ecossaise and the Ph.D. award I was granted in 2010; to the Institut Pierre Renouvin (Paris I-Sorbonne); to the Maison Française D'Oxford (January 2006 grant) and to the GRHIS research group at Rouen University.

I would like to express my thanks to my editors Jenny McCall and Holly Tyler for their professionalism, their patience and their thoroughness.

Personally, I would like to thank my supervisors Professors Robert Frank and Catherine Maignant for having supported and encouraged me ever since I started my research on the subject of Irish immigration into Scotland. I am also deeply grateful to Dr Martin Mitchell, who has read and commented on my work for the past 10 years. I would also like to express my deepest gratitude to Professors Thomas M. Devine, Callum Brown, John

DOI: 10.1057/9781137329844

Foster, Bernard Aspinwall, Gérard Noiriel and Jacques Leruez, who gave me useful comments and guidelines throughout my research.

My remarkable teachers and professors Joëlle Boyer, Pierre-Alain Rogues and Pierre Albertini passed onto me their passion for history – this work is a humble homage from their pupil and student.

My deepest thanks go to all who have corrected and improved the English version of this book, namely Claire Sanderson, Myriam Boussahba-Bravard, Elise Trogrlic, Marius Hentea, Jack Dunn, Constance Bantman and Joe Cunningham.

My father Patrick Vaughan spent innumerable hours (re)reading and correcting the manuscript. His English is above perfection, and any errors are mine.

I convey my gratitude to all my friends and colleagues who read the French version of the Ph.D. dissertation: Anne Bellouin, Anaïs Fléchet, Bernard Ludwig, Jenny Raflik, Olivier Compagnon, Olivier Feiertag, Colombe de Dieuleveult. My Rouen colleagues and friends have shown strong moral support: I would like to thank, especially, Anne Besnault and Florence Cabaret. I am also indebted to Arnaud Brennetot for his expertise in mapping.

During my long research stays in Scotland, my Scottish family welcomed me to a second home: warm thanks to Aileen Vaughan, Tony McIlwham, Ciaran and Nicole for their generous hospitality. I would also like to thank my mother, my husband, Hadrien France-Lanord, and my children Lysandre and Pierre, for their constant love and support.

My grandfather, Michael Vincent Vaughan, was the most genial and loveable Irish immigrant I have ever met – without him, I would never have started writing on the subject. This work is a tribute to his teachings and to his love.

DOI: 10.1057/9781137329844

List of Abbreviations

AC	*The Airdrie and Coatbridge Advertiser*
CD	*The Catholic Directory*
CE	*The Coatbridge Express*
CL	*The Coatbridge Leader*
FP	*The Glasgow Free Press*
GA	*The Greenock Advertiser*
GAA	Glasgow Archdiocese Archives
GCA	Glasgow City Archives
GE	*The Glasgow Examiner*
GH	*The Greenock Herald and General Advertiser*
GO	*The Glasgow Observer*
GT	*The Greenock Telegraph and Clyde Shipping Gazette*
NAS	National Archives of Scotland
NLA	North Lanarkshire Archives
PP	Parliamentary Papers
SCA	Scottish Catholic Archives

DOI: 10.1057/9781137329844

Map of Western Scotland

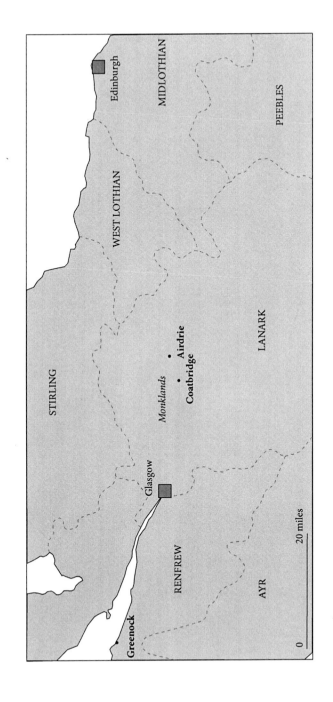

palgrave▶**pivot**

www.palgrave.com/pivot

Introduction

Vaughan, Geraldine. *The 'Local' Irish in the West of Scotland, 1851–1921*. Basingstoke: Palgrave Macmillan, 2013. DOI: 10.1057/9781137329844.

▶

Irish travelling to Scotland in the nineteenth century have often been portrayed as 'emigrants of despair' – in contrast with the 'emigrants of hope' crossing the Atlantic.[1] Far from being a *terra incognita*, Scotland had been a familiar destination for Irish migrants since early modern times. The children of Erin had crossed over to Scotland as seasonal agricultural labourers, as linen artisans helping to develop the textile industry or as Presbyterian students attending Scottish universities.[2] Yet the rate of Irish migration to Scotland accelerated at the time of the Great Famine: in 1841, the Irish-born represented 4.8 per cent of the Scottish population. By 1851, the Irish population reached its peak at 207,367, corresponding to 7.2 per cent of Scotland's inhabitants.

Defining the nature of Irish migration remains a delicate task. Were the Irish *migrants* or *immigrants* into Scottish society? The term *immigration* makes sense if a nation-state exists with defined borders and has a clear legal definition of nationality.[3] The invention of the word *immigrant* was concomitant with the American Revolution, namely the birth of a modern nation which decided who could enter (*in–migrare*) the country. From this perspective, since the Irish were subjects of the United Kingdom, moving from their native land to Scotland can be considered as a simple migration, unless Scotland is considered a (stateless) nation. From a legal standpoint, the Irish were British subjects (1800 Act of Union) and were not submitted to the Registration of Aliens Act (1836). However, the language of official authorities was ambiguous – the 1871 Census Report defined them as 'the most numerous *aliens* in Scotland', and local authorities sometimes also referred to the Irish poor as 'aliens'.[4] This terminology had to do with Ireland's particular standing within the British identity, as Protestants still considered Catholics as being, in some ways, 'outlandish'.[5]

In his major work *The Uprooted*, Oscar Handlin wrote: 'Once I thought to write a history of the immigrants in America. Then I discovered that the immigrants *were* American history.'[6] Similarly, one could say that the history of the Irish in Scotland shaped the history of modern Scotland. Effectively, the Irish interacted with the three traditional pillars of Scottish identity: religion, education and the law. From a religious perspective, the Irish Catholics represented a threat to Presbyterian Scotland, especially at a time when the religious landscape was fragmented. Whereas the Church of Scotland had to struggle in the face of the Disruption (1843) and the rise of the dissenting churches, Roman Catholics showed an apparent united stance.[7] As far as education is

DOI: 10.1057/9781137329844

concerned, after the passing of the Education Act (1872), Irish Catholics became a perceived threat to Scottish representatives on local school boards and a disruptive element in the definition of Scottish education. By maintaining a separate schooling system, the Catholics made a stand against the spirit of Presbyterian 'public schools' (where the Shorter Catechism was taught).[8] As regards the law, the Irish poor, Catholics and Protestants alike, represented a threat to the judicial system in that they brought into question the administration of the Poor Law (1845) and of the poorhouses. Thus, the Irish, by taking up arms against the essential values of Scottish identity, forced the Scots to reappraise and put forward *what made Scotland Scotland*.[9] In this respect, the Irish certainly acted as 'enlighteners' of Scotland's national identity in the nineteenth century.

This book offers to revisit the ways in which the Irish adapted to and helped fashion their Scottish environment as well as how the Scots reacted to the regular waves of incomers. It proposes to adopt a local perspective on Irish and Scottish issues of identities, whether religious, political, or social. Up until now, the Irish Catholic conquest of local municipal and parochial institutions has been rather neglected by the historiography on the Irish in Britain. In order to understand the distinctiveness of this phenomenon, retracing the evolution of historical writings on the Irish in Britain over the past 40 years is a necessary first step.

The history of Irish immigration to Great Britain became a subject of interest to British historians mainly from the late 1970s. Along with the turmoil surrounding 'The Troubles' in Northern Ireland, there emerged a public debate on Britain's multicultural society.[10] The post-colonial perspective also influenced historical studies on Ireland in the early 1980s as some historians began to consider the Irish as colonial subjects both inside and outside of Ireland. The portrait of the typical Irish migrant, which historians started to carve out in the early 1980s, was that of a single, male, lower working-class, Catholic and rejected individual. This first type of approach echoed nineteenth-century portraits (such as the one sketched by Engels in his study of Manchester in 1844), and pioneer studies like that of J.A. Jackson who had written that 'the Irishman's clothes, his brogue and general appearance, even when he was not speaking in Gaelic, singled him out from the rest of the community as an outsider, a stranger in the midst'.[11]

This singularity of the Irish migrant was highlighted in Sheridan Gilley and Roger Swift's first edited collection on the subject *The Irish in the Victorian City* (1985), in which M.A.G. O'Tuathaigh's essay on the

DOI: 10.1057/9781137329844

problematic integration of the Irish in Britain set the general tone for a series of urban studies of Irish communities (including essays on Bristol, York, Liverpool, Wolverhampton, and Stockport in England; Glasgow and Edinburgh in Scotland).[12] Alongside these local explorations of the Irish in various towns, Swift and Gilley's second collection of essays *The Irish in Britain 1815–1939* (1989) adopted a more global perspective on the sons and daughters of Erin living in Great Britain.[13] David Fitzpatrick's opening contribution stressed 'the curious middle place' of Irish migrants in Britain, who were neither 'an expatriate community [n]or a fully accepted ingredient of British community'.[14]

The early 1990s thus witnessed a move towards a more balanced approach of Irish migrants, which called for studies going beyond 'poverty, Catholicism and drink'.[15] Graham Davies' book *The Irish in Britain 1815–1914* (1991), epitomized how issues of spatial integration, work, religious diversity and the Irish migrants' local/national political involvement (Chartism for instance) were key to Irish migration studies.[16] Davies insisted on the fundamental diversity of the Irish experience in Britain according to the various places of settlement. The migratory process was characterized by the multiplicity of manifestations of Irishness as well as the range of British reactions to these several generations of migrants. His research embodied an 'integrationist' approach according to which anti-Irish feeling in Britain faded in the late Victorian era (a view largely criticized by historians such as Donald MacRaild).

Thus, within a decade, from the early 1980s to the 1990s, the image of the typical Irish migrant in Britain had begun to change. New explorations started to bear witness to the existence of rural migrants alongside the industrial navvies, with Protestant Billies and Margarets standing next to Catholic Paddies and Biddies, as well as lower-middle class migrants.[17] In addition, historians of the Irish in Britain also departed from an essentially local and national point of view, to capture the essence of Irishness in Britain set in a global diasporic context. This challenge was taken up for instance in Patrick O'Sullivan's edited collection *The Irish World Wide* (six volumes published between 1992 and 1997), with chapters on the Irish in the British metropole and abroad. Such thematic approach reflected growing interests within academia on themes such as gender (volume four); and issues of identity (volumes three and five) with the study of autobiographies, filmography and music. In a similar approach, Andy Bielenberg's edited volume *The Irish Diaspora* (2000) used a comparative world perspective on the Irish migrants' experience. It also

DOI: 10.1057/9781137329844

introduced a feature as yet under-developed, that of the importance of Irish migrants within the British Empire.[18] Accordingly, revisionist historians and disciples of the school of New Imperial History revolutionized the perception of the Irish migrant as a colonizer and imperial agent in the British colonies.[19]

During the past 40 years, the image of the Irish in Britain has considerably changed: first studied as ill-fitted migrants struggling in urban settings, the Victorian and Edwardian Irish in Britain now appear as complex figures cutting across religious and social boundaries. Accordingly, the year 2010 opened with the publication of another volume edited by Swift and Gilley, *Irish Identities in Victorian Britain*.[20] Compared to their preceding collections, the title reveals how the academic perspective has shifted from studying the Irish in their environment and urban setting ('city', 'Britain', 'locality') to focusing on self-representations and perceptions – as Swift and Gilley put it 'the paradox… that in order to preserve their Irishness, the Irish also had to change it'.[21] The essay in this study by Alan O'Day on 'mutative ethnicity' in a transnational context epitomizes new trends in the historiography of the Irish in Britain.[22] The agenda is also set for new studies that should inquire into 'the social, cultural and political milieu within which the Irish middle class operated in nineteenth-century Britain, particularly on a provincial level'.[23] In the most recent general study of the Irish in Britain (2011), Donald MacRaild paves the way for a new decade of research. Along with the now traditional study of economic, religious, spatial and assimilation issues, newer ventures are examined, such as the role of women in Orangeism, and also a more global outlook on gender and ethnicity. His overall argument is that the historian should trace both changes and continuity in Britain's different generations of Irish.

How does the historiography of the Irish in Scotland fit into this broader British picture? Roger Swift reminds us how Scottish historians such as John McCaffrey helped researchers explain Scottish issues by 'concentrating on forces within Scottish society, viewed within a Scottish context'.[24] Others have demonstrated the importance of Irish immigration – which 'forms one of the most significant themes of modern Scottish history'.[25] Scotland's centuries-long connection with Ulster certainly entailed an early interest in the study of Irish migration to Caledonia. The first synthesis on *The Irish in Scotland 1798–1845* was published by James Edmund Handley in 1943. This portrayal of the Irish community in Scotland was thoroughly researched and made way for

DOI: 10.1057/9781137329844

later studies on Irish settlement, ways of life, sectarianism, employment and integration issues. Yet case studies of particular Irish communities really took off in the 1970s.[26]

In contrast with research south of the border, the historiography of the Irish in Scotland has developed three main areas of investigation: religion (and its sectarian offspring), politics and employment. In terms of religious conflict, Tom Gallagher's *Glasgow: The Uneasy Peace* (1987) explored the extent of sectarianism in Glasgow from the nineteenth century and the assimilation of Irish migrants in the late twentieth century. In Thomas Devine's edited collection *Irish Immigrants and Scottish Society* (1991), the Catholic community was explored by Bernard Aspinwall, William Sloan, and Tom Gallagher.[27] 'Continuity and a *devotional* watershed' characterized Irish religious practice according to Aspinwall who has thoroughly explored all aspects of Irish Catholic devotion ever since.[28] In his chapter on Irish Catholics in the West of Scotland, Martin Mitchell (2008) reassessed the outcast figure of the Irish Catholic migrant.[29]

The importance of Irish Protestant immigration to Scotland was initially underlined by Graham Walker (1991), who demonstrated that Irish Protestants represented at least a quarter of the total number of Irish migrants.[30] This study echoed political and associational aspects of Protestant Irish immigration, which had already been explored by Elaine McFarland in her synthesis on nineteenth-century Orangeism.[31] The most recent research on the subject of Irish Protestantism in Scotland by Ian Meredith has demonstrated that the growth of the Episcopalian Church in Victorian Scotland was a result of Irish Protestant migration.[32] Amongst the Irish Protestants settling in Scotland, John Ferguson (1836–1906), born in Belfast the son of a Presbyterian father and Episcopalian mother, migrated to Glasgow in 1859.[33] Ferguson was one of the key organizers of the Irish nationalist movement in Scotland.[34] In terms of political activity, earlier participation of the Irish migrants in national politics was examined by Martin Mitchell, who stressed their positive influence on Scottish radical political campaigns.[35] In this respect, there lacks a general history of the Irish workforce in Scotland, but there are local studies or studies of Irish workers as part of the Scottish labour force, such as the masterly works by Alan Campbell on Scottish miners.[36]On the whole, since the 1950s, the history of the Irish in Scotland has evolved – the outcast, religiously segregated, strike-breaking and politically apathetic Irish have turned into multifaceted individuals. The impact of Irish Protestantism, the political involvement of Irish communities and their

DOI: 10.1057/9781137329844

participation in Scotland's industrial boom throughout the nineteenth century is at the heart of contemporary scholarship. In the most recent collection on Irish destinies in Scotland, Mitchell called for 'more local studies of the Catholic Irish... examining individual Catholic communities in depth.'[37]

This book aims to answer this call, for both Catholic and Protestant Irish migrants. Major Scottish cities such as Glasgow, Edinburgh or Dundee have already been examined by historians, whereas my intention is to reduce the observation scale by resorting to the tools of microhistory. By proceeding in this way, new perspectives emerge, as demonstrated by Giovanni Levi: 'Phenomena previously considered to be sufficiently described and understood assume completely new meanings by altering the scale of the observation.'[38] Consequently, this book focuses on three medium-sized towns in the West of Scotland: Greenock, Airdrie and Coatbridge – a port and two mining towns. Greenock was an ancient royal burgh, whose destiny was closely linked to the Glasgow municipality: in 1851, the city had 37,000 inhabitants (a tenth of Glasgow's population).[39] In the Monklands, a region lying ten miles east of the industrial capital, the barony burgh of Airdrie, a mining town, had 12,000 dwellers in 1851 whereas Coatbridge, which was legally defined as a village, had a population of over 8,000 that same year.[40] These three towns were all industrial cities, attracting Irish workers: shipbuilding and sugar refineries dominated in Greenock, while mining and iron-making were major activities in the Monklands. They have also been selected because of their common history of sectarianism. For instance, in July 1835, violent fights between Irish Catholics and Orangemen resulted in a death in Airdrie; in February and July 1851, the street preaching of the Angel Gabriel, a zealous predicator, provoked an attack on the presbytery and the Catholic church in Greenock.[41] Furthermore, vestiges of a sectarian past are still evident today – 'whilst religious ghettoisation has been much reduced in Glasgow, in surrounding towns it is still significant – even perhaps heightened by council-letting policy in towns like Greenock, Port Glasgow, Airdrie and Coatbridge', wrote Callum Brown in 1997.[42]

The purpose of this book is both to reassess and to disclose new perspectives on Irish identity and religion as well as Irish political involvement in the West of Scotland. The role played by the churches in the formation of Catholic and Protestant identities needs to be reconsidered (especially Mary Hickman's claims relative to the

DOI: 10.1057/9781137329844

'denationalizing' enterprise of the Catholic Church) by stressing the elaboration and multiplicity of religious associations (friendly societies, parochial societies and so on) as well as the importance of the schooling issue.[43] On Irish involvement in politics, Richard McCready wrote that 'The Irish, both Catholic and Protestant, have played a major role in Scottish politics. In many respects this has been portrayed in simplistic terms and more detailed analysis is required.'[44] Accordingly, this book considers it crucial to review the writings on the participation of the Irish in parliamentary elections, and also to focus on a long-neglected issue, that of *Irish participation in local politics* – because 'Scottish control was still paramount where it mattered most to people in the Victorian period, that is at the level of the city, the burgh, the locality'.[45] Perhaps, then, Scotland should not be considered as this 'stateless nation' when, effectively, the municipal decision-makers or local instances of power escaped British management. It was precisely within those local boards that Scottish conceptions of power in the making were revealed. The fact that the Irish already sat on local boards in the early 1850s, notably the parochial boards (where the area of the parish defined the political territory), was certainly a sign that the Irish had already penetrated a true Scottish institution.

Fighting against historiographical biases which still persist in the literature on the subject is also fundamental. For instance, the poverty and mobility of the migrants need be reassessed. The Irish are still too often defined as a 'tramping people', a migratory and poor people. Of course, no one could deny that in Scotland the Irish were overwhelmingly deprived, changing location according to available work – but seldom have the small urban Irish elites been studied.[46] In fact, entering local politics implied a series of criteria which few Irish could meet: spare time, sufficient wealth and geographical stability were requisite to contest local elections. When some of the Irish succeeded in being elected to these local boards, it was possible to hear *Irish voices* speaking in the name of their people in these municipal councils, whereas the majority of the Irish remain, for the historian, a *voiceless* people. One could argue that the words spoken by a few Irish upstarts should not be taken into account – yet those Irish councillors were in fact defending the rights of their deprived countrymen. Another stereotypical argument is that nationalism acted as a barrier to the rise of local preoccupations. Irish nationalism was very strong in the West of Scotland, and some of the local prominent Irishmen, such as Charles

DOI: 10.1057/9781137329844

O'Neill in Coatbridge (a close friend of John Ferguson's), were key figures in the West of Scotland nationalist movement. In fact, both local
and nationalist political involvement were politicization factors for the
middle class Irish – for, pursuing a career within the nationalist movement could serve municipal purposes and vice versa (O'Neill being
a perfect example of this local/nationalist combination). Building a
political network for parliamentary and municipal elections, and prac-
tising public debate within Irish leagues or local councils, helped the
Irish familiarize themselves with the political scene. Furthermore, local
interests should not be contrasted with national or nationalist purposes
since local councils had to deal with national decisions (by enforcing
them or by sending petitions to Parliament for instance), and also
because nationalists were particularly sensitive to all that concerned
the *nation* whether it be the Scottish or the Irish nation (occasionally
one finds Irish councillors giving their Scottish counterparts lectures
on patriotism). Lastly, the study of Irish involvement in local politics
has been hindered by the idea that in Catholic communities the power
of the priests prevented individual political initiative – hence, William
Walker, in his study on Dundee, argued that the priests' power was similar to that of a Communist Party secretary in the USSR.[47] The Catholic
clergy's influence was indeed great, especially in educational matters
(priests were elected to School Boards from 1873), and when access to
poorhouses was requested by priests to keep Irish Catholics away from
Protestant influence (in the 1850s and 1860s). But this authority should
not be overestimated: divisions within the Catholic Church (disputes
between the hierarchy and the clergy or fights between Scottish and
Irish priests) did weaken the priests' political zeal; certain areas of local
life were rarely of interest to the clergy. In addition, the laity's capacity
to react to overbearing clergy must not be underrated. Some Catholic
laymen did make their debut in local political life by struggling against
their own clergymen – a fact for which they were often admired by
their Scottish fellow citizens. Conversely, the Irish could also make use
of the parochial political network (halls for meetings, electoral lists)
for their local campaigning.

The time period chosen is that of the *long-time span,* dear to Fernand
Braudel, focusing on 'groups, collective destinies and general movements', expanding over 70 years, between 1851 and 1921.[48] The first
modern census in Scotland was undertaken in 1851: at this point in
time, the number of people born in Ireland reached its peak. The year

DOI: 10.1057/9781137329844

1921, ending with the signing of the Anglo-Irish treaty marked a legal and symbolic change in the nature of Irish migration to Scotland. The war years are therefore included in this book in order to examine whether the 'suspended time' which the 1914–18 period represented put a stop to or accelerated the settling of the Irish migrants and their descendants. Studying three towns together is by no means what Marc Bloch defined as 'comparative history', because the history of the Irish in these different areas represents 'fractions of the same society which is defined, as a rule, by its overwhelming unity'.[49] The perspective taken by this book is rather to offer a variation of scales and magnitudes relating to the same phenomenon, in which each city presents micro-changes occurring within the broader framework of the Scottish nation.

To perceive and analyse the varying destinies of the Irish in these three towns, different sources ranging from official documents to personal accounts have been examined. Yet lack of literacy and poverty amongst the majority of immigrants account for the relative scarcity of individual testimonies. Instead, historians have to rely mainly on the vast amount of information available in local newspapers.[50] Notwithstanding the fact that this type of source represented the view of the better-off Scots, it is nevertheless one of the only platforms where the deprived Irish could be seen and heard. For instance, court reports often transcripted the words of some poor son of Erin with his distinctive brogue.[51] In that respect, judicial archives such as the examinations in the High Court of Edinburgh also give a unique perspective on how Irish witnesses or defendants talked and expressed their views.[52] From a Catholic perspective, the letters sent by Irish and Scottish priests to the Glasgow Vicariate (subsequently the Archdiocese) or the personal diaries of some Irish clergymen (such as Michael Condon in Greenock) are also accounts of the lives of the Irish in a 'strange land'. The Catholic press gives us further information concerning Irish friendly societies and Irish nationalist local sections.[53]

This book thus revisits issues concerning the religion and politics of the Irish immigrants in a local context. Its ultimate ambition is to shed new light on local political identities by focusing on a group long neglected, namely Irish urban élites in small Scottish towns. By exploring Irish lives in a local context, the purpose is not to narrow down the investigation but rather to demonstrate how these Irish connected to larger national and British issues.

DOI: 10.1057/9781137329844

Notes

1 See D. MacRaild (2011) *The Irish Diaspora in Britain, 1750–1939* (Basingstoke: Palgrave Macmillan), pp. 189–200.

2 G. Walker (1991) 'The Protestant Irish in Scotland' in T.M. Devine (ed.) *Irish Immigrants and Scottish Society in the Nineteenth and Twentieth Centuries* (Edinburgh: John Donald), pp. 45–6.

3 G. Noiriel (1998) 'La Tyrannie du National' in J.-C. Ruano-Borbalan (ed.) *L'identité: L'individu, le groupe, la société* (Auxerre: Sciences Humaines Editions), pp. 289–96; G. Noiriel (1988) *Le Creuset français. Histoire de l'immigration XIXe-XXe siècle* (Paris: Seuil), pp. 71–124.

4 PP, Eight Decennial Census of the Population of Scotland taken April 3d 1871 with Report, p. XXXIV; *AC*, 28 June 1872.

5 L. Colley (1992) 'Britishness and Otherness: An Argument', *The Journal of British Studies*, 31, pp. 309–29; L. Colley (1992) *Britons. Forging the Nation 1707–1837* (London: Yale University Press), p. 23.

6 O. Handlin (1951) *The Uprooted: The Epic Story of the Great Migrants that Made the American People* quoted by D. MacRaild (1999) *Irish Migrants in Modern Britain, 1750–1922* (London: Macmillan Press), p. 2.

7 See T. Gallagher (1987) *Glasgow: The Uneasy Peace: Religious Tension in Modern Scotland* (Manchester: Manchester University Press).

8 Some Irish Protestants can be included in this third remark, as the Episcopalian Church also maintained separate schools on account of their refusal to teach the Shorter Presbyterian Catechism.

9 Walter Scott quoted by T.M. Devine (2000) *The Scottish Nation 1700–2000* (London: Penguin), p. 286.

10 Although there had been pioneer studies such as J. A. Jackson's (1963) *The Irish in Britain* (London: Routledge). Social historians such as E.P. Thompson (1964) also contributed to the historiography of the labouring Irish *The Making of the English Working Class* (New York: Vintage Books), pp. 429–43). For a literature review on the subject of Irish migrants in Britain, see Roger Swift's various contributions since the early 1980s: R. Swift (1993) 'The Historiography of the Irish in Nineteenth Century Britain: Some Perspectives' in P. Buckland and J. Belchem (eds) *The Irish in British Labour History. Conference Proceedings in Irish Studies, 1* (Liverpool: Institute of Irish Studies), pp. 8–12; R. Swift (2000) 'Historians and the Irish: Recent Writings on the Irish in Nineteenth-Century Britain' in D. MacRaild (ed.) *The Great Famine and Beyond: Irish Migrants in Britain in the Nineteenth and Twentieth Centuries* (Dublin: Irish Academic Press), pp. 14–39.

11 J. A. Jackson (1963) *The Irish in Britain*, p. 154.

12 One of the precursors of a revisionist vision of Irish integration into British mainstream society was R. J. Cooter who completed an M.A. thesis at

DOI: 10.1057/9781137329844

Durham University in 1972. His work was published in 2005: *When Paddy Met Geordie. The Irish in County Durham and Newcastle 1840–1880* (Sunderland: The University of Sunderland Press). The late 1970s and early 1980s saw urban explorations of the Irish communities: see Lynn Hollen Lees (1979) *Exiles of Erin. Irish Migrants in Victorian London* (Manchester: Manchester University Press); F. Finnegan (1983) *Poverty and Prejudice: A Study of Irish Immigrants in York, 1840–1875* (Cork: Cork University Press).

13   In terms of geographical coverage, another collection of essays edited by R. Swift and S. Gilley (1999) *The Irish in Victorian Britain. The Local Dimension* (Dublin: Four Courts Press) presented the migrants in different urban settings (Stafford, Hull, Birmingham and London for instance) but also in different counties (Cornwall, Lancashire and the South West), thus introducing its readers to the rural Irish workforce.

14   D. Fitzpatrick (1989) 'A Curious Middle Place: The Irish in Britain, 1871–1921' in R. Swift and S. Gilley (eds) *The Irish in Britain, 1815–1939* (London: Pinter), p. 11.

15   D. MacRaild (1999) *Irish Migrants,* p. 5.

16   G. Davies (1991) *The Irish in Britain 1815–1914* (Dublin: Gill and Macmillan).

17   A. O'Dowd (1991) *Spalpeens and Tattie Hokers: History and Folklore of Irish Migratory Agricultural Workers in Ireland and Britain* (Dublin: Irish Academic Press); P. O'Sullivan (1995) *Irish Women and Irish Migration* (London: Leicester University Press).

18   A. Bielenberg (2000) 'Irish Emigration to the British Empire, 1700–1914' in A. Bielenberg (ed.) *The Irish Diaspora* (Harlow: Pearson), pp. 215–34.

19   K. Kenny (ed.) (2004) *Ireland and the British Empire* (Oxford: Oxford University Press); S. Howe (2000) *Ireland and Empire. Colonial Legacies in Irish History and Culture* (Oxford: Oxford University Press). Transnational connections in the Irish diaspora have been examined in D. MacRaild (ed.) (2000) *The Great Famine and Beyond,* pp. 1–13. As stated by Kevin Kenny (2006), comparative history ought to 'transcend the nation-state as the primary unit of analysis, searching for reciprocal interactions and the sensibilities they nurture among globally scattered communities' in K. Kenny 'Symposium: Perspectives on the Irish Diaspora', *Irish Economical and Social History*, XXXIII, p. 40.

20   The contributions had originally appeared in 2009 issue of *Immigrants & Minorities*, 27. R. Swift and S. Gilley (eds) (2010) *Irish Identities in Victorian Britain* (London: Routledge).

21   R. Swift and S. Gilley (2009) 'Introduction', *Immigrants & Minorities*, 27, p. 132.

22   A. O'Day (2009) 'Conundrum of Irish Diasporic Identity: Mutative Ethnicity', *Immigrants & Minorities*, 27, pp. 317–39.

23   R. Swift (2009) 'Identifying the Irish in Victorian Britain: Recent Trends in Historiography', *Immigrants and Minorities*, 27, p. 146.

DOI: 10.1057/9781137329844

24   R. Swift (2000) 'Historians and the Irish: Recent Writings on the Irish in Nineteenth-Century Britain', in D. MacRaild (ed.) *The Great Famine and Beyond*, p. 32.

25   T.M. Devine (ed.) (1991) *Irish Immigrants*, p. V.

26   See, for instance: J. McCaffrey (1970) 'The Irish Vote in Glasgow in the Later Nineteenth Century: A Preliminary Survey', *The Innes Review*, 21, pp. 30–6; W. Walker (1972) 'Irish Immigrants in Scotland: Their Priests, Politics and Parochial Life', *The Historical Journal*, XV, pp. 649–67; S. Gilley (1980) 'Catholics and Socialists in Glasgow, 1906–1912' in K. Lunn (ed.) *Hosts, Immigrants and Minorities – Historical Responses to Newcomers in British Society 1870–1914* (Folkestone: Dawson), pp. 160–200. ; I. S. Wood (1980) 'John Wheatley, the Irish and the Labour Movement in Scotland', *Innes Review*, 31, pp. 71–85; B. Aspinwall (1982) 'The Formation of the Catholic Community in the West of Scotland', *Innes Review*, 33, pp. 44–57; A. Campbell (1979) *The Lanarkshire Miners, A Social History of their Trade Unions, 1775–1874* (Edinburgh: John Donald); B. Collins (1978) *Aspects of Irish Immigration Into Two Scottish Towns (Dundee and Paisley) During the Mid-Nineteenth Century*, unpublished Ph.D. thesis, University of Edinburgh.

27   T. Gallagher (1991), 'The Catholic Irish in Scotland: In Search of Identity' in T. Devine (ed.) *Irish Immigrants and Scottish Society*, pp. 19–43; B. Aspinwall (1991), 'The Catholic Irish and Wealth in Glasgow' in T.M. Devine (ed.), *Irish Immigrants*, pp. 91–115. See also T. Devine (ed.) (1996) *St Mary's Hamilton. A Social History 1846–1996* (Edinburgh: John Donald).

28   B. Aspinwall (2008) 'Catholic Devotion in Victorian Scotland' in M.J. Mitchell (ed.) *New Perspectives on the Irish in Scotland* (Edinburgh: John Donald), p. 31. See also: B. Aspinwall (1992) 'Children of the Dead End: the Formation of the Archdiocese of Glasgow, 1815–1914', *The Innes Review*, 43, pp. 119–44; B. Aspinwall (1996) 'Scots and Irish Clergy Ministering to Immigrants, 1830–1878', *The Innes Review*, 47, pp. 45–68.

29   M.J. Mitchell (2008) 'Irish Catholics in the West of Scotland in the Nineteenth Century: Despised by Scottish Workers and Controlled by the Church?' in M.J. Mitchell (ed.) *New Perspectives*, pp. 1–19.

30   G. Walker (1991) 'The Protestant Irish in Scotland' in T. Devine (ed.) *Irish Immigrants and Scottish Society*, pp. 44–66.

31   E.W. McFarland (1990) *Protestants First. Orangeism in 19th Century Scotland* (Edinburgh: Edinburgh University Press).

32   I. Meredith (2008) 'Irish Migrants in the Scottish Episcopal Church in the Nineteenth Century' in M.J. Mitchell (ed.), *New Perspectives*, pp. 44–64; I. Meredith (2009) 'Irish Episcopalians in the Scottish Episcopal Diocese of Glasgow and Galloway during the Nineteenth Century', *Immigrants & Minorities*, 27, pp. 248–78.

DOI: 10.1057/9781137329844

33   E.W. McFarland (2003) *John Ferguson, 1836–1906: Irish Issues in Scottish Politics* (East Linton: Tuckwell Press); E. W. McFarland (2009) 'The Making of an Irishman: John Ferguson (1836–1906) and the Politics of Identity in Victorian Glasgow' in *Immigrants & Minorities*, 27, pp. 194–211.

34   J. McCaffrey (1970) 'The Irish Vote in Glasgow in the Later Nineteenth Century: A Preliminary Survey', *The Innes Review*, 21, pp. 30–6; J. McCaffrey (1979) 'Politics and the Catholic Community since 1878' in D. McRoberts (ed.) *Modern Scottish Catholicism 1878–1978* (Glasgow: J. Burns), pp. 140–55; J. McCaffrey (1988) 'Irish Immigrants And Radical Movements in the West of Scotland in the Early Nineteenth Century', *Irish Review*, 29, pp. 46–60. See also I.S. Wood (1975) 'Irish Nationalism and Radical Politics in Scotland 1880–1906', *Journal of the Scottish Labour History Society*, 9, pp. 21–38; A. O'Day (1979) 'Irish Home Rule and Liberalism' in A. O'Day (ed.) *The Edwardian Age: Conflict and Stability, 1900–1914* (London: Macmillan), pp. 113–32; T. Gallagher (1981) 'Catholics in Scottish Politics', *Bulletin of Scottish Politics*, 1, pp. 21–43. See also R. McCready (1998) 'Irish Catholicism and Nationalism in Scotland: The Dundee Experience, 1850–1922', *Irish Studies Review*, 6/3, pp. 245–52.

35   M.J. Mitchell (1998) *The Irish in the West of Scotland, 1797–1848: Trade Unions, Strikes and Political Movements* (Edinburgh: John Donald).

36   A.B. Campbell (1979) *The Lanarkshire Miners, A Social History of their Trade Unions, 1775–1874* (Edinburgh: John Donald); A.B. Campbell (2000) *The Scottish Miners 1874–1939, vol. 1: Industry, Work and Community* (Aldershot: Ashgate); A.B. Campbell (2000) *The Scottish Miners 1874–1939, vol. 2 : Trade-Unions and Politics* (Aldershot: Ashgate). See also: W. Sloan (1991) 'Religious Affiliation and the Immigrant Experience: Catholic Irish and Protestant Highlanders in Glasgow, 1850' in T.M. Devine (ed.) *Irish Immigrants*, pp. 67–90. The Irish mill workers in Dundee were also studied by William Walker (1973) *Juteopolis: Dundee and Its Textile Workers 1885–1923* (Edinburgh: Scottish Academic Press). See also: R.B. McCready (2003) 'The Social and Political Impact of the Irish in Dundee, c.1845–1922', unpublished Ph.D. thesis, University of Dundee. Physical force nationalist movements in Scotland have been studied by Mártín O'Catháin (2008) 'A Winnowing Spirit: Sinn Féin in Scotland, 1905–1938' in M.J. Mitchell (ed.) *New Perspectives*, pp. 114–26; M. O'Catháin (2007) *Irish Republicanism in Scotland, 1858–1916. Fenians in Exile* (Dublin: Irish Academic Press).

37   M.J. Mitchell (2008) 'Irish Catholics in the West of Scotland' in M.J. Mitchell (ed.) *New* Perspectives, p. 19. See also R. Swift (1993) 'Devine, Irish Immigrants and Scottish Society', *Irish Historical Studies*, XXVIII, p. 454.

38   G. Levi (1991) 'On Microhistory' in P. Burke (ed.) *New Perspectives on Historical Writing* (Cambridge: Polity Press), p. 98.

DOI: 10.1057/9781137329844

39 R.D. Lobban (1971) 'The Irish Community in Greenock in the Nineteenth Century', *Irish Geography*, VI, pp. 270–81. Lobban's perspective was essentially economic and geographic.

40 The Irish in the Monklands have not yet been studied in a published case study. See Ann M. McDonagh (nd.) 'Irish Immigrants and Labour Movements in Coatbridge and Airdrie, 1891–1931', B.A. Honours Dissertation, University of Strathclyde.

41 Airdrie Library, U27/0458: *The History of Airdrie and Poems* by the late William McHutchinson, tinsmith, Baird and Hamilton, Airdrie; U27/0065: meeting of the Airdrie town council (21 July 1835) whereby the total amount of urban damage is of £44. Concerning the Greenock incidents, see: *GT*, 18 February 1851 and J. E. Handley (1947) *The Irish in Modern Scotland* (Cork: Cork University Press) p. 95. A sectarian reputation lingered in the Monklands where in 1994 the 'Monklandsgate' scandal displayed 'highly publicised accusations that Catholic members of the ruling Labour group on Monklands District Council operated sectarian policies in providing jobs for relatives and in concentrating public expenditure on the Catholic parts of the district'. Nepotism rather than sectarianism were evidenced, yet this scandal epitomized the survival of sectarian feelings in the Monklands. See S. Bruce (1996) 'Review: Political and Cultural Interaction Between Scotland and Ulster', *Scottish Affairs*, 15 (http://www.scottishaffairs.org/backiss/pdfs/sa15 /sa15_Bruce.pdf, date accessed 15 December 2012).

42 C. Brown (1997) *Religion and Society in Scotland since 1707* (Edinburgh: Edinburgh University Press), p. 195.

43 M.J. Hickman (1992) 'Incorporating and Denationalizing the Irish in England: The Role of the Catholic Church' in P. O'Sullivan (ed.) *The Irish World Wide, vol. 5: Religion and Identity* (London: Leicester University Press), pp. 196–216.

44 R.B. McCready (2000) 'Revising the Irish in Scotland' in A. Bielenberg (ed.) *The Irish Diaspora*, p. 44.

45 T.M. Devine (2000) *The Scottish Nation*, p. 217.

46 D. Fitzpatrick (1989) 'A Peculiar Tramping People: The Irish in Britain, 1801–1870' in W.E. Vaughan (ed.) *A New History of Ireland. Vol. V: Ireland Under the Union, I, 1801–1870* (Oxford: Clarendon Press), pp. 623–60. The middle class Irish have been studied by Bernard Aspinwall (for Scotland) and John Belchem. See B. Aspinwall (1982) 'The Formation of the Catholic Community in the West of Scotland', *Innes Review*, 33, pp. 44–57; and J. Belchem (2005) 'Priests, Publicans and the Irish Poor: Ethnic Enterprise and Migrant Networks in Mid-Nineteenth-Century Liverpool', *Immigrants and Minorities*, 23, pp. 207–31.

47 W.M. Walker (1972) 'Irish Immigrants in Scotland: Their Priests, Politics and Parochial Life' *The Historical Journal*, XV, pp. 649–67. Mitchell has

DOI: 10.1057/9781137329844

questioned this argument; see M.J. Mitchell (2008) 'Irish Catholics' in M.J. Mitchell (ed.) *New Perspectives*, pp. 1–19.

48   See O. Harris (2004) 'Braudel: Historical Time and the Horror of Discontinuity', *History Workshop Journal*, 57, pp. 161–74; F. Braudel (1949) *La Méditerranée et le monde méditerranéen à l'époque de Philippe II. Vol. 2: Destins collectifs et mouvements d'ensemble* (Paris: Armand Colin).

49   M. Bloch (1928) 'Pour une histoire comparée des sociétés européennes' in *L'histoire, la guerre, la résistance* (Paris: Gallimard, 2006), p. 350.

50   Amongst which there were: *The Airdrie and Coatbridge Advertiser, The Coatbridge Express, The Coatbridge Leader* for the Monklands, *The Greenock Telegraph and Clyde Shipping Gazette* in Greenock.

51   See Edward Muir's introduction in E. Muir and G. Ruggiero (eds) (1991) *Microhistory and the Lost Peoples of Europe. Selections from Quaderni Storici* (London: John Hopkins University Press), p. XVI.

52   NAS, series AD/14 (Lord Advocate's Department).

53   *The Free Press* (1851–1868) and then *The Glasgow Observer* and *The Glasgow Examiner*. Further official documents include parliamentary commissions on the Irish poor and on religious education; manuscripts of census enumerators and census reports; minute books of the various local boards (school boards, parochial boards and town councils).

DOI: 10.1057/9781137329844

1

Tracking Down the Irish

Abstract: *Chapter 1 opens with a geographic and urban portrait of Airdrie, Coatbridge and Greenock. There follows an overall picture of Irish migrants in the Monklands and Greenock using the 1851, 1871, 1901 and 1911 census evidence (with systematic samples allowing the exploration of family patterns and the establishment of comparisons between the occupational profiles of Highlanders, Lowlanders and Irishmen). Whereas Irish Catholics could be clearly identified in Scotland, Irish Protestants have been considered to be more 'invisible'. Yet, by a careful examination of local prison registers which recorded religious affiliations, this chapter argues that, whilst on the one hand, Irish Protestant religious affiliations differed from the Scottish ones, on the other hand, Catholic and Protestant occupational profiles were quite similar.*

Vaughan, Geraldine. *The 'Local' Irish in the West of Scotland, 1851–1921.* Basingstoke: Palgrave Macmillan, 2013. DOI: 10.1057/9781137329844.

One of the most notable features of Irish migration to Scotland was the steady flow of migrants throughout the Victorian era.[1] In 1851, at the climax of the migration movement, 207,367 Irish-born lived in Scotland – 7.2 per cent of the total population (compared with 2.9 per cent in England). In 1901, there were still 205,064 Irish-born recorded in Scotland, although their proportion had decreased to 4.6 per cent (3.3 per cent in 1921).[2]

Alongside traditional seasonal agricultural migrants, Victorian Scotland's growing industrial sector needed a low-paid workforce – for 'Irish settlement reflected the pull of job opportunities at least as much as the push of home circumstances'.[3] Back in the 1820s, the Glasgow press readily complained of 'the cheapness with which this Class of persons get over from Ireland to Scotland in the steam boats threaten[ing] to overwhelm the west of Scotland with the miserable beings in the lowest state of wretchedness and want'.[4] In fact, early nineteenth-century rural Irish immigrants had settled in the South West (Wigtonshire and Kircudbrightshire) whereas industrial workers headed for Ayrshire, Renfrewshire and Glasgow where weavers and navvies were required.[5] In his pioneering study of the Irish in Scotland, Handley indicated how the Irish had contributed to the 'enormous expansion of the population of Lanarkshire in the nineteenth century' which increased from 146,699 in 1801 to 530,169 in 1851, with Glasgow itself numbering 344,986 that same year.[6] The Irish-born represented 13 per cent of the county's population in 1841. In neighbouring Renfrewshire, one-tenth of the population was Irish-born, overwhelmingly concentrated in Paisley, Renfrew, Port Glasgow and Greenock.[7]

Departing from Glasgow, trains transported migrants to the 'magnet' villages and towns of the Monklands, a coal and ironstone mining region lying only a few miles east.[8] In its centre was the town of Airdrie, a town which had acquired the status of Parliamentary burgh in 1832 and of Municipal burgh in 1849.[9] Irish migrants had come to settle in the early nineteenth century to work in the town's linen industry – but the increasing number of migrants in the 1840s reflected a change in the nature of industrialization, namely 'the ascendancy of heavy industry over agriculture and handloom weaving'.[10] In 1841, Father Daniel Gallagher of Airdrie reported to a Parliamentary commission that a third of the Irish settlers worked in mines whereas 54 per cent of them worked as general labourers.[11] Ten years later, in 1851, the Airdrie population reached 25,000 (five times its recorded 1821 population). Similarly, Coatbridge rose from

DOI: 10.1057/9781137329844

being a village of 741 inhabitants in 1831 to a town of over 8,000 in 1851. The Baird brothers developed the mining of the local blackband ironstone in Coatbridge and its neighbourhood.[12] In 1841, the Parliamentary Inquiry on mining gave a vivid description of this industrial town on the rise:

> At night, ascending to the hill on which the established church stands, the groups of blast furnaces on all sides might be imagined to be blazing volcanoes, at most of which smelting is continued on Sundays and weekdays, by day and night, without intermission.[13]

Further west, on the banks of the River Clyde, trade with the British colonies had contributed to the commercial and industrial growth of Greenock since the eighteenth century. In the early 1830s, as many as 4,000 Irish migrants were employed in the town's various industries:

> the rest are labouring men, many of whom work at the quays, loading and unloading vessels; others are engaged by the farmers... a good many work as ship carpenters; a great many are engaged in the sugar factories; some in the foundries.[14]

The town had 37,000 inhabitants in 1851, roughly a tenth of the Glaswegian population. Although Greenock's success as a trading port was declining by the 1850s, its industries connected to the naval trade prospered, with a steadily growing number of sugar refineries, rope works and shipbuilding yards.[15] The port of Greenock served Irish migrants disembarking from the steamers as well as a great number of Scots emigrating to the New World. This illustrated what T. M. Devine has identified as the 'Scottish emigration paradox'.[16] As a consequence, the harbour area was a place of tension, a symbol for many contemporaries of Scotland's 'talent drain' as well as what could be perceived as the 'invasion' of the sons and daughters of Erin. One result of this situation was the 1855 anti-Catholic riots which started off on the steps of the Steam Boat Quay, where John Orr (known as the 'Angel Gabriel') excited a mob, an event which led to several days of religious upheaval.[17]

The census evidence

In the Monklands, the arrival of the Irish was sometimes interpreted as an 'occupation' of Scottish territory, as reported in the local press:

DOI: 10.1057/9781137329844

'Go, for us, into any of our towns and villages – our own amongst the rest – and inquire or look around you, and it will be frequently difficult to say whether you are in Scotland or in Ireland'.[18] This statement exaggerated the actual numbers of Irish residents. In 1851, the Airdrie Sheriff Archibald Alison stated that 15,000 Irish lived in the Monklands (out of a population of 50,000). The census samples of Airdrie and Coatbridge in 1851 indicate that a third of the inhabitants were Irish-born. In Airdrie, by 1861, the Irish represented 18.5 per cent of the total population. As regards Irish Catholics, Father Michael O'Keeffe counted 6,395 parishioners in 1868 (40 per cent of Coatbridge's population).[19] According to decennial censuses, the proportion of Irish-born in Airdrie's population decreased from 14.2 per cent in 1871 to 12.1 per cent in 1891 – however, if the second-generation Irish are taken into account, the Irish community represented a third of the urban population in the early 1890s.[20] In Coatbridge, according to the 1871 census sample, a third of all urban dwellers was born in Ireland. However, by 1891, the 4,793 Irish-born constituted only 19.7 per cent of Coatbridge's inhabitants (24,320), but taking into account the second-generation, the Irish community still represented around 40 per cent of the urban population.[21] The growth of the Catholic population was undeniable, with 7,527 Catholics present in Coatbridge in 1874 (which represented an 18 per cent increase since 1868).[22]

In Greenock, the 1841 census reported 4,307 Irish in the town, namely 11.7 per cent of the urban population. But the proportion of Irish-born in Greenock had strongly increased by the early 1870s: the 1871 Census report estimated that 'of the Eight Principal Towns of Scotland, Aberdeen contained the lowest proportion of Irish-born, Greenock the highest'.[23] Following this increase, the proportion of Irish-born slightly decreased from 16.5 per cent in 1871 to 12.4 per cent in 1891. Nevertheless, if the birth-rate is taken into account, the Irish community in Greenock during the 1871–91 years formed around 25 per cent to 30 per cent of the urban population. As regards the Irish Catholic population, the yearly census conducted by Father Michael Condon in the parish of Saint Lawrence indicated that there was a 20 per cent increase in the 1869–84 period (the number of Catholics reached 3,256 in 1884).[24]

Irish immigration to Scotland was a continuing phenomenon in the prewar period, although the number of first generation Irish was slightly decreasing (Table 1.1).

DOI: 10.1057/9781137329844

TABLE 1.1   *Irish-born in Airdrie, Coatbridge and Greenock, 1901–11*

Census Year	Irish-born in Airdrie	Irish-born in Coatbridge	Irish-born in Greenock	% of Irish-born in Airdrie	% of Irish-born in Coatbridge	% Irish-born in Greenock
1901	2,325	4,688	7,509	10. 4%	12.7%	11%
1911	1,980	4,592	6,678	8.1%	10.6%	8.9%

Source: 1901 & 1911 Census of Great-Britain (Scotland).

Occupational profiles

A random systematic sample was drawn from the manuscript censuses of Airdrie and Coatbridge in 1851. As a result, Irish and Scottish occupational profiles in the adult population (over 15 years of age) can be contrasted.[25] The classification adopted, inspired by W. A. Armstrong, defines five classes (Appendix 1), ranging from professionals and elites (Class I) to skilled categories (Class III: artisans and skilled workers), to semi-skilled (Class IV) and unskilled workers (Class V).[26]

In comparison with the Scottish workforce, the Irish dominated Class V in Airdrie (Figures 1.1 and 1.2). In Coatbridge, the Irish were few in the highest profiles of employment (Class II for instance). The bulk of Erin's sons and daughters were to be found in semi-skilled and unskilled categories, as carriers, carters, furnace keepers, coal labourers, pit bottomers (Class IV) and general labourers, watchmen, hawkers, and so on (Class V). Within Classes IV and V, a third of the Irish were employed in coal and iron mines, as Alan Campbell explained in his study of the Lanarkshire miners: 'Ironstone…was harder to cut… It was therefore easier for Irishmen to get employment at the more arduous and unpleasant work of ironstone mining.'[27] He also calculated that almost half of the miners in Coatbridge in 1851 were Irish.[28] Nevertheless, the most common figure of the Irish working man in the Monklands in the 1850s was that of the navvy: 70 per cent of those who declared 'labourer' as a profession in the census were Irish.

Examined by the parliamentary inquiry of 1834, Father Gordon of Saint Mary's, Greenock, declared that the Irish were mainly labourers, although there were 'a few small shopkeepers, some clothes merchants,

DOI: 10.1057/9781137329844

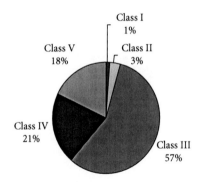

FIGURE 1.1   *Irish workers in Airdrie, 1851*
Source: 1851 Census of Great Britain.

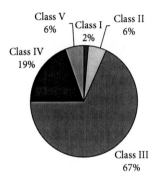

FIGURE 1.2   *Scottish workers in Airdrie, 1851*
Source: 1851 Census of Great Britain.

some brokers, and some provision sellers. Many of them are also hawkers'.[29] In 1851, the Irish formed a fifth of Greenock's population: with a sample drawn from this census (1,176 people), the professional status of Lowlanders, Highlanders and the Irish can be established (Figure 1.3).

According to Figure 1.3, the Irish were at the bottom of the social pyramid of employment in Greenock, with 65 per cent of them being in the lowest grades (Classes IV and V) of employment, although it was also the case that Highlanders were not to be found either in the highest classes (over 50 per cent in Classes IV and V). The Greenock female workforce (263 working women in the sample) was mostly employed in domestic trades (40 per cent) as seamstresses (14 per cent), textile workers (9 per cent) and

DOI: 10.1057/9781137329844

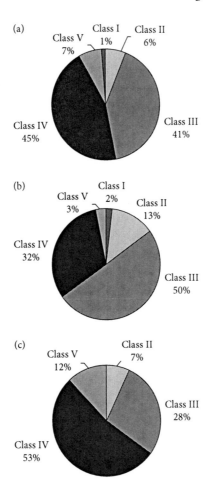

FIGURE 1.3   *(a), (b) and (c) Occupational profiles of Highlanders (a), Lowlanders (b) and Irish (c) in Greenock, 1851*

Source: 1851 Census.

washerwomen (5 per cent). By contrast, there were fewer servants amongst the Irish female workforce (27 per cent as opposed to 40 per cent) but there were a greater number of mill girls (27 per cent) who had 'acquired their occupational skills and crafts in the Ulster linen industry'.[30]

The same pattern of employment continued to prevail in the early 1870s Monklands. Thus half of the Irish workforce was in unskilled and semi-skilled trades according to the 1871 census sample. Compared to the Scottish working population, the Irish were proportionately

DOI: 10.1057/9781137329844

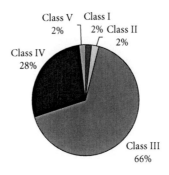

FIGURE 1.4   *Second-generation Irish workforce in Airdrie, 1871*
Source: 1871 Census of Great Britain.

over-employed in the lowest trades. Effectively, they were seldom to be found in the highest occupations (Classes I and II) and their occupational profile within these classes was thinly spread (essentially spirit dealers), whereas the Scots were present as industrial managers, factory directors, musicians, and so on. Moreover, a closer look at Class III reveals further discrepancies between the Irish and the Scots: whereas 60 per cent of the Irish belonging to this class were miners, only 21 per cent of Scots were (the majority being artisans).

However, second-generation Irish faired slightly better than their forebears: their social classification was closer to the Scottish class distribution (figure 1.4). The Irish born in Scotland were thus more numerous than the Irish-born in skilled trades (66 per cent of the former versus 45 per cent of the latter).[31] Nevertheless, social mobility and intergenerational mobility were limited. In neighbouring Coatbridge, three quarters of the working Irish belonged to Classes IV and V whereas only 43 per cent of the Scottish workforce were in these categories of employment in 1871. Similarly, in Greenock, 45 per cent of first generation Irish in 1891 were employed in unskilled and lower skilled trades.[32] Whereas the Irish represented 1 per cent of Classes I and II in 1851, they still formed no more than 2.4 per cent of those categories in 1891.

The 1911 Census report investigated occupational profiles according to place of birth, and gave a general picture of Irish-born employment in Scotland:

> The proportion of general labourers in the Irish-born section of the population is found to be much higher than either in the entire population or

DOI: 10.1057/9781137329844

in the English and Welsh-born sections of the population; the ratio in the Irish-born section is 67.8 per thousand of the occupied males, while the corresponding figure in the entire population and in the English and Welsh-born section of the population are per thousand 23.2 and 19.7 respectively.[33]

Additionally, the Irish continued to be over-represented amongst the poor and vagrants: in 1901, the census of migratory poor in Airdrie indicated that out of 21 homeless persons, 15 had been born in Ireland.[34] In 1911 amongst 97 vagrants enumerated in Coatbridge, 42 were Irish.[35] 'Greenock's navvy poet' as the *Greenock Telegraph* nicknamed Patrick McGill, portrayed the arrival of Irish navvies in the mid-1900s:

> The potato merchant met us on Greenock quay next morning, and here Micky's Jim marshalled his squad, which consisted in all of twenty-one persons. Seventeen of these came from Ireland, and the remainder were picked up from the back streets of Greenock and Glasgow.[36]

McGill, a.k.a. Dermod Flynn, worked as a seasonal harvester before getting hired as a manual labourer on several building sites. His lodgings in Glasgow mirrored the housing crisis in early twentieth century Scotland:

> I got a job on the railway and obtained lodgings in a dismal and crooked street...The landlady was an Irishwoman, bearded like a man, and the mother of several children... We slept in the one room, mother, children and myself... Manual labour was now becoming irksome to me, and eight shillings a week to myself at the end of six days' heavy labour was poor consolation for the danger and worry of the long hours of toil.[37]

Added to census evidence, it must be concluded that intergenerational social mobility was limited until the First World War, for 'as the first generation faded, there was evidence of social mobility. But most of that occurred within the working class, not out of it.'[38]

The invisibility of Irish Protestants reassessed

Irish Protestant immigration was particularly strong in Scotland, as over 80 per cent of Irish emigrants came from one of the nine counties of Ulster.[39] This Ulster–Scottish connection was centuries old and was strengthened in the eighteenth century by Irish Presbyterian students who came to study at Glasgow and Edinburgh universities as well as by linen

DOI: 10.1057/9781137329844

artisans such as weavers and bleachers who taught their techniques to the Scottish workforce.[40] The historical nature of this Ulster–Scottish link, as Donald MacRaild puts it, may partly explain the 'invisibility' of Irish Protestant migrants.[41] Another sound indicator of Irish Protestant presence was the great development of the Orange Order.[42] In Airdrie, the first Loyal Orange Lodge (No. 19 Purple Heroes) was opened in 1824 – within a decade, lodges were also created in Greenock, with Greenock Orangemen taking part in the 12th of July demonstrations organized in Glasgow.[43]

From a religious perspective, how 'invisible' were Irish Protestants in a Presbyterian land? Generally, these migrants belonged to the Presbyterian, Methodist and Episcopalian denominations.[44] The usual estimate would be that around half of the Protestant immigrants were Presbyterian, the other half belonging to the Episcopalian Church and various Dissenting Chapels (Free Church of Scotland, United Presbyterian, and Methodist). In the case of Episcopalians, Ian Meredith has pointed out correlation between the influx of Irish migrants and the construction of new churches.[45] Although there can be no accurate estimate of the religious affiliation of these migrants, yet a method can be devised based on the examination of prison registers, which give details of nationality and religion (the Airdrie and Greenock prison housed large numbers of prisoners serving negligible sentences for minor offences).[46]

Interestingly, the Greenock Prison Registers seem to corroborate Ian Meredith's assumptions on the Irish and the Episcopalian Church in Scotland – 'given such a large working class membership, and the propensity of the Irish for petty crime, it would be expected that the proportion of Episcopalians in prison in the Glasgow area would be high'.[47] In Greenock prison, amongst 84 Irish prisoners (in 1858), 32 were Protestants, including 14 Episcopalians, ten Kirk of Scotland churchgoers, and eight Dissenting Presbyterians (Figure 1.6). The high proportion of Episcopalians was connected to the early existence of an Episcopalian Church in Greenock (1823) built for English and Irish parishioners. This overrepresentation of the Anglican faith amongst the Irish Protestants certainly made them stand apart from their Presbyterian hosts (Figure 1.5).

Information obtained from the Airdrie prison register (Figure 1.8) in 1848 showed that out of a total of 113 Irish-born prisoners, 33 were Protestant (29 per cent of the total number of prisoners), of which ten gave their religion as being 'Protestant', twenty as 'Presbyterian', two as 'Free Church' and one as 'Episcopalian'.[48]

DOI: 10.1057/9781137329844

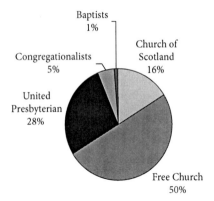

FIGURE 1.5   *Protestants denominations in Greenock, 1851*
Source: Religious census of Great Britain, 1851.

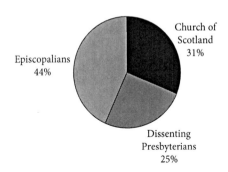

FIGURE 1.6   *Irish Protestants in Greenock prison, 1858*
Source: NAS, HH/21 prison register, 1858.

Protestant religious affiliation was thus flexible amongst Irish-born prisoners, as a third of them declared they belonged to no specific Protestant church (Figure 1.8). The majority of Irish prisoners in Airdrie (62 per cent) belonged to the Established church. This affiliation with the Kirk did not necessarily help them blend into Airdrie's religious landscape as there were only a fifth of Protestants who belonged to the Established Church (Figure 1.7).[49] The smaller proportion of Episcopalians amongst

DOI: 10.1057/9781137329844

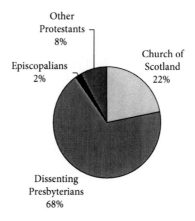

FIGURE 1.7   *Protestant denominations in Airdrie, 1851*
Source: Religious census of Great Britain, 1851.

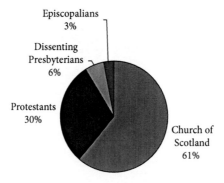

FIGURE 1.8   *Irish Protestants in Airdrie prison, 1848*
Source: NAS, HH/21: Airdrie prison register, 1848.

Irish Protestants in Airdrie might be explained by the specific ritualistic nature of the Episcopal Church in Scotland: much later, in 1912, Bishop Jenkins wrote that the Irish immigrant regarded the Scottish Episcopal Church in the Glasgow diocese as 'papistical'.[50]

Interestingly, the prison registers also provided information on occupation and literacy, allowing the historian to establish a comparison between Irish Catholics and Protestants. Figure 1.9 reveals an identical

DOI: 10.1057/9781137329844

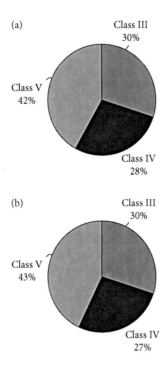

FIGURE 1.9   *(a) and (b) Occupational profiles of Irish Catholics (a) and Irish Protestants (b) in Airdrie Prison, 1848*

Source: NAS, HH/21: Airdrie prison register, 1848.

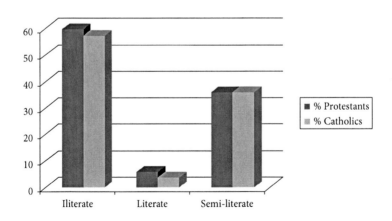

FIGURE 1.10   *Irish prisoner literacy in Airdrie Prison, 1848*

Source: NAS, HH/21: Airdrie prison register, 1848.

DOI: 10.1057/9781137329844

professional outline for Irish Catholics and Protestants; also, the literacy figures (classified in three categories: literate, illiterate and 'semi-literate' for those who could either read or write a little) confirm the similarity of Irish profiles.

This similarity of Irish Protestant and Catholic destinies corroborates John Foster's conclusions on the Clydeside Irish, and Graham Walker's remarks on the fact that 'our image of the Irish poor category in nine-teenth century Glasgow has neglected the Protestant element'.[51] However, in slight contrast with the Airdrie prisoners, skilled workers (Class III) were more numerous amongst the Greenock Irish Protestant prisoners (16 per cent against 10 per cent of the Irish prisoners) – as can be seen from Figure 1.11.

Furthermore, concerning Class V, half of the Irish Catholic prisoners fit into this category while only a third of the Irish Protestant prisoners did – the literacy figures also confirmed the Protestants' slight social lead on their Catholic counterparts.

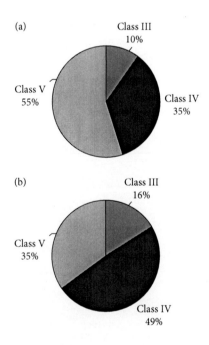

FIGURE 1.11   *(a) and (b) Occupational profiles of Irish Catholics (a) and Irish Protestants (b) in Greenock prison, 1858*

Source: NAS, HH/21: Greenock prison register, 1858.

DOI: 10.1057/9781137329844

On the whole, 'small differences' appear to have existed between the Irish Catholic and Protestant workers, and this fact was already obvious in the eyes of certain contemporaries – such was the case with Father Tracy of Pollockshaws, who stated before a 1870 Parliamentary inquiry: 'It is commonly understood that the Irish paupers are all Roman Catholics. I wish to say that only about half of them are Catholics.'[52] When the commission's chairman asked him: 'is that a proportion that we may assume to be general throughout Scotland of the Irish population?', the priest answered as thus: 'I think so, especially in Glasgow, in the whole of the west.'[53]

Conclusion

What made the Irish migrants 'stand apart' from their Scottish counterparts? As the censuses indicated, a great number of the sons and daughters of Erin were unskilled and semi-skilled workers but then Scots, both Highlanders and Lowlanders, were also chiefly employed as labourers in the three overwhelmingly industrial towns under study. However, a close analysis of Greenock's census reveals how 'small differences' existed between the Irish and other migrants such as the Highlanders who also came from a chiefly Catholic peasant background. The most striking fact was the diversity of Irish migrant experience – they came from different religious backgrounds and filled in a variety of social occupations, whatever their denomination. If the unskilled dominated the Irish workforce, there were nevertheless also skilled workers and craftsmen, both men and women, who crossed over the Channel. The Irish migrants could not be narrowed down to simply being a 'tramping people'. What kept them distinct from their Scottish hosts was a form of Irish identity, imagined by both migrant and host communities, a point which will be further developed in Chapter 2.

Notes

1   B. Collins (1991) 'The Origins of Irish Immigration to Scotland in the Nineteenth and Twentieth Centuries' in T. Devine (ed.) *Irish Immigrants and Scottish Society in the Nineteenth and Twentieth Centuries* (Edinburgh: John Donald), p. 1.

DOI: 10.1057/9781137329844

2   These figures do not include subsequent Irish generations born in Scotland of Irish parentage, but this issue will be discussed further down.

3   B. Collins (1991) 'The Origins of Irish Immigration', p. 11.

4   *Glasgow Courrier*, 10 June 1824; GCA, TD546/3/11, p. 7.

5   G. Walker (1991) 'The Protestant Irish in Scotland' in T. Devine (ed.) *Irish Immigrants,* p. 48.

6   J. E. Handley (1964) *The Irish in Scotland* (Glasgow: John Burns), p. 52.

7   J. E. Handley (1964) *The Irish in Scotland,* p. 49.

8   J. E. Handley (1964) *The Irish in Scotland,* p. 52.

9   See P. Drummond (1987) 'Place Names of the Monklands' (Airdrie: Monkland Library Services); GCA: TD 729/53, 'Airdrie, a brief historical sketch', p. 12.

10   GCA, TD750/53, 'Airdrie, a brief historical sketch', p. 17.

11   Aidrie Local History Room: *Saint Margaret's Airdrie 1836–1936* (Glasgow: John S. Burns & Sons printers), 1936, p. 6.

12   James B. Neilson's hot blast process (1830) permitted the extraction of ironstone. See P. Drummond and P. Smith (eds) *Coatbridge: Three Centuries of Change,* Monklands Library Services Department, p. 33.

13   P. Drummond and P. Smith (eds) *Coatbridge,* p. 19.

14   F. M. Dunlop (2001) *St Mary's Greenock. The Story of a Community* (Greenock: St Mary's Publishing), p. 42.

15   R. D. Lobban (1971) 'The Irish Community in Greenock in the Nineteenth Century', *Irish Geography,* VI, p. 270.

16   T.M. Devine (1995) *Exploring the Scottish Past. Themes in the History of Scottish Society* (East Lothian: Tuckwell Press), pp. 238–39.

17   NAS, AD 14/55/280: 1855 High Court indictment vs. Robert McEwan, Neil McPhaill, Malcom Morrison and Lachlan Cameron, for mobbing and rioting.

18   *AC*, 10 March 1864.

19   GAA, GC/1/16/3: 'Census of the Coatbridge Mission, September 1869'. Since Coatbridge was by status a village in the 1860s, the proportion of Irish was not available in the census reports. The Irish Catholics in Greenock were less numerous: in the mid-1830s, the Catholic parish of Saint Mary's included 3,950 Irish parishioners.

20   This conservative estimation was calculated with the average Scottish birth-rate. The 1871 census sample of Airdrie indicates that 27.5 per cent of the urban population were first and second-generation Irish.

21   GAA, GC/76: *History of the Missions of the Archdiocese (1901),* p. 82. In Coatbridge, the Archdiocese estimated in 1901 a population of 14,000 Catholics, amounting to a third of the city's inhabitants.

22   GAA, GC/1/16/3: Letter from Michael O'Keeffe to Vicariate, September 1869; GC/7/3/1: Letter from Michael O'Keeffe to Vicariate, 10 March 1875 ('Statement in reference to the Coatbridge and Whifflet Missions').

DOI: 10.1057/9781137329844

23 PP, *Eight Decennial Census of the Population of Scotland Taken April 3rd 1871 with Report.* p. XXXIV.
24 CD (1884), p. 110.
25 Random systematic sample of 7.7 per cent of the adult population over 15 taken from the *Census Enumerators' Bookscripts*, New Monkland (parish 651) 1851 E.D. 1–16; E.D. 17–33; Old Monkland (parish 652): 1851 E.D. 1–8; E.D. 9–35; E.D. 36–5. See Wendy Gordon's methodology (2002) *Mill Girls and Strangers. Single Women's Independent Migration in England, Scotland, and the United States, 1850–1881* (Albany: State University of New York), pp. 167–70.
26 W. A. Armstrong (1972), 'The Use of Information about Occupation' in E. A. Wrigley (ed.) *Nineteenth-Century Society: Essays in the Use of Quantitative Methods for the Study of Social Data* (London: Cambridge University Press), pp. 191–310. The classification of miners was problematic: thus, the 'colliers', 'iron miners' and coal miners' were put in Class III (skilled occupation) whereas 'miners' or 'coal labourers' were classified in Class IV (semi-skilled). See Appendix 1.
27 A. B. Campbell (1979) *The Lanarkshire Miners, A Social History of their Trade Unions, 1775–1874* (Edinburgh: John Donald), p. 179.
28 A.B. Campbell (2000) *The Scottish Miners 1874–1939, vol. 1: Industry, Work and Community* (Aldershot: Ashgate), p. 321.
29 F. M. Dunlop (2001) *Saint Mary's Greenock. The Story of a Community*, p. 42.
30 R.D. Lobban (1971) 'The Irish Community in Greenock', p. 273.
31 When trying to analyse second-generation social mobility, we assumed that second-generation 'Irish' were children born in Scotland of Irish parentage. However, the researcher must be cautious since this definition denoted an imperialistic vision of Irishness, conveyed by Irish nationalists. In his famous autobiography *The Life Story of an Old Rebel* (Dublin), John Denvir, an Irishman living in Britain, stated that 'anyone who has mixed much among our fellow-countrymen in England, Scotland or Wales knows that, generally, the children and grandchildren of Irish-born parents consider themselves as much Irish as those born on the "old sod" itself' (p. 2).
32 R. D. Lobban (1971) 'The Irish Community in Greenock', p. 270.
33 PP, *Report on the Twelfth Decennial Census of Scotland (1911)*, vol. III, 1913, p. VIII.
34 *AC*, 29 June 1901.
35 *CL*, 1 July 1911.
36 *GT*, 29 December 1914; P. McGill (1914) *Children of the Dead End* (Edinburgh: Birlinn, 2001), p. 77.
37 P. McGill (1914) *Children of the Dead End*, pp. 267–68.
38 See D. MacRaild (2011) *The Irish Diaspora in Britain, 1750–1939* (Basingstoke: Palgrave Macmillan), p. 60.
39 A. B. Campbell (1979) *The Lanarkshire Miners*, p. 182; B. Collins (1991) 'The Origins of Irish Immigration', p. 14. According to our 1851 Census sample, in the Coatdyke area (part of Coatbridge), 62 per cent of the 218

DOI: 10.1057/9781137329844

recorded Irish-born came from Ulster (counties Roscommon, Antrim, and Tyrone).

40   G. Walker (1991) 'The Protestant Irish', p. 47. In 1861, 49 per cent of Ulster inhabitants were Protestants.

41   D. MacRaild (1999) *Irish Migrants in Modern Britain, 1750–1922* (London: Macmillan Press), p.101.

42   See Chapter 2.

43   *AC*, 17 July 1875; *AC*, 14 July 1883. By the late 1870s, there were five lodges in Airdrie (n°19 Purple Heroes; n°125 Evening Star, n°181 Victoria Lodge and n°230 Caledonian Lodge) and 12 in Coatbridge.

44   C.G. Brown (1990) 'Each Take Off their Several Way? The Protestant Churches and the Working Classes in Scotland' in G. Walker and T. Gallagher (eds) *Sermons and Battle Hymns: Protestant Popular Culture in Modern Scotland* (Edinburgh: Edinburgh University Press), p. 76.

45   I. Meredith (2008) 'Irish Migrants in the Scottish Episcopal Church in the Nineteenth Century' in M.J. Mitchell (ed.), *New Perspectives on the Irish in Scotland* (Edinburgh: John Donald), p. 45. Although there were counter-examples such as the Episcopalian Church of Coatbridge (Saint John's) built in the early 1840s, and designed to accommodate 'southern workmen', that is the English migrant population (yet its first rector, the Reverend Kennedy, was himself an Irishman). See NLA, U40/1/9/24: *A Concise History of St. John's Church, Coatbridge (1893)*.

46   See the method used by J. Foster, M. Houster and C. Madigan (2002) 'Distinguishing Catholics and Protestants among Irish Immigrants to Clydeside: A New Approach to Immigration and Ethnicity in Victorian Britain', *Irish Studies Review*, 10/2, pp. 171–92.

47   I. Meredith (2008) 'Irish Migrants in the Scottish Episcopal Church', p. 267.

48   NAS, HH21/46/001.

49   Callum Brown remarked that socially, it was not surprising that the proportion of Presbyterian dissidents should be weak amongst Irish Protestant working men given that, for instance, in the 1850s and the 1860s, practices (in the Free and United Presbyterian Churches) such as 'fencing the table' were applied to prevent people morally or socially suspicious from going to these churches.

50   I. Meredith (2008) 'Irish Migrants in the Scottish Episcopal Church', p. 58.

51   J. Foster (2002) 'Distinguishing Catholics and Protestants', p. 187; W. Graham (1991) 'The Protestant Irish', p. 56.

52   PP, 1870 (357) XI.1: Report from the Select Committee on Poor Law (Scotland), p. 194.

53   PP, 1870 (357) XI.1: Report from the Select Committee on Poor Law (Scotland), p. 194.

DOI: 10.1057/9781137329844

2
Irishness(es)

Abstract: *Chapter 2 assesses what types of analytical categories help us better understand how the Irish stood as immigrants in their Scottish host society. By attempting a definition at a local level, it contributes to the ongoing debate on the influence of an official anti-Irish racism which determined British attitudes to the Irish politically and socially. It will be argued that when racialization of the Irish did occur, it did not determine all the reactions of Scottish local élites towards their Irish counterparts. Another specific Scottish issue, which has received wide coverage in the press in recent years, is that of sectarianism. In seeking to define precisely what this term meant, Chapter 2 will undertake to analyse the scope of sectarian attitudes and their chronological variance.*

Vaughan, Geraldine. *The 'Local' Irish in the West of Scotland, 1851–1921*. Basingstoke: Palgrave Macmillan, 2013. DOI: 10.1057/9781137329844.

Identity can be defined by a twofold paradigm. First, identity is a process and not a permanent state, and second, it is not 'a mechanical constancy, an indefinite repetition of same but it is dialectical, in that it integrates the other in the same and change in continuity'.[1] Thus, otherness is an essential component of identity – implying that Scottishness also helped shape the identity of the Irish residing in Scotland. Trying to define Irishness the way it emerged in Scotland is a delicate task, because it is hard to differentiate between Scottish prejudices and the distinctiveness of the Irish. Should it be attempted to separate Scottish perceptions from Irish insights? Sheridan Gilley has argued, for instance, that the Paddy stereotype was both a British and an Irish design.[2] As a result of the scarcity of Irish testimonies on their own conceptions of their identity in Scotland, researchers tend to be left with the Scots' views on what it meant to be Irish in this 'strange land' of adoption. Moreover, how did Scottishness and Irishness relate to the 'dominant' identity in the United Kingdom, i.e. Britishness? Linda Colley has demonstrated that British identity could not be ascribed to an English colonization of the Celtic fringes.[3] Thus, the flexibility of Britishness allowed various national, provincial and local identities to co-exist. Protestantism and the Empire were common references for all Britons – except for Irish Catholics (although they participated in the building of the Empire).[4] Evidently, it was difficult for Ireland, as an overwhelmingly Catholic country with certain colonial features, to fit into this general definition of Britishness.[5] Nevertheless, Irish Protestants who emigrated to Scotland claimed to be British and not Irish.[6]

Victorian Irish identities

Irish identity in Victorian Scotland was a complex blend of nationalist ideals, Protestant and Catholic Irish images combined with Scottish perceptions of the Irish. It can first be examined through the connection with the mother country, since migrants were asked for their 'place of birth' during census enumeration, or when they petitioned for poor relief.[7] Crossing the Irish Sea did not cost much: accordingly, some of them returned to their native town or village (often when a child was going to be born, as can be observed in the census books); others were reminded of their homeland on Saint Patrick's day – for instance, when pictures and slide shows were available in the late Victorian era, exiles could get a glimpse of the

DOI: 10.1057/9781137329844

green hills of Erin. However, the geographical criterion defining identity becomes less valid when examining second-generation 'Irish' who, in most cases, had never set foot on their parent's native isle. The linguistic criterion, if considered as a component of Irish identity, is less convincing for the Irish living in Scotland: the great majority of the migrants were bilingual (Irishmen asking for interpreters in court, for instance, was a very rare occurrence). Rather than Gaelic being a distinctive feature, it was the Irish brogue that was mocked by the Scots – journalists reporting court dialogues did not need to state that a person who pronounced diversion *divershun* or who said *plase yer honor* was Irish.[8]

Concerning the influence of religion in the making of identity, the notion that Catholic and Irish were interchangeable terms in the Victorian vocabulary has been criticized. This is a late nineteenth-century vision stemming from the fact that, as historians have demonstrated, the Catholic nationalists 'hijacked' the term Irish in one of the 'greatest imperialist coups of the 19th century'.[9] It must be kept in mind that Scottish contemporaries often distinguished between the Protestant and Catholic Irish, although during tense political periods, like the 'Fenian panic' of the 1860s for instance, Irish and Irish Catholic nationalists were equated in public discourse.

Irishness was thus constructed by the immigrants themselves and also by Irish gazing into the Scottish mirror. Thus, it was both an Irish and a Scottish creation, and there is no point in imagining an immutable Irishness, unresponsive to Scottish variations in perceptions. The identity of the Irish, as was the case for their ethnicity, was defined by its plasticity and adaptability. It was both 'the way in which members of a national, racial or religious grouping maintain an identity with people of the same community in a variety of official and unofficial ways', and 'not an indelible stamp impressed on the psyche but a dimension of individual existence that can be consciously emphasized or de-emphasized as the situation requires'.[10]

Is 'race' a satisfying category of analysis?

The debate over the racialization of the Irish in Britain has being lively in academia during the past 30 years. Among its main protagonists, the American historian Lewis P. Curtis, and, albeit in different terms, Mary Hickman and M. A. G. Ò Tuaithaigh on the other side of the Atlantic,

DOI: 10.1057/9781137329844

have all argued that there existed a form of Anglo-Saxon racism directed against the 'Celtic' Irish.[11] As Curtis reasserted in a recent comment article (2005), this anti-Irish racism, which of course needs to be defined beyond skin pigmentation, determined British political responses and attitudes to 'white' Irish people (both in and outside of Ireland).[12] Yet the advocates of a revisionist approach to the racialization perspective have not denied the expression of certain racist attitudes.[13] When looking at mid-Victorian Scotland, there were certainly occurrences and expressions of forms of racism, emanating from official instances as well as from Scottish citizens, against the Irish migrants.

An oft-quoted 'classic' instance of the racialization of the Irish appears in Friedrich Engels' *The Condition of the Working Class in England* (1844). He wrote of '[t]hese Irishmen who migrate for fourpence to England... And even if the Irish, who have forced their way into other occupations, should become more civilized, enough of the old habits would cling to them to have a strong, degrading influence upon their English companions in toil.'[14] This quote gives readers a sense of how the Irish were in some cases regarded as an inferior 'race', with a pessimistic outlook on their chances of becoming civilized. Degradation and contagion of the British native class by this migrant *lumpen proletariat* worried Socialists and the State for different reasons – Engels' concern related to the negative influence exerted by Irish migrants on a future workers' revolution. Scottish authorities manifested another kind of angst, as can be seen in the report accompanying the census returns of 1871:

> This very high proportion of the *Irish race* in Scotland has undoubtedly produced deleterious results, lowered greatly the moral tone of the lower classes, and greatly increased the necessity for the enforcement of sanitary and police precautions.[15]

As in Engels' quote, the vocabulary associated with Irish migrants relate to race, class, physical and moral depravation. There is much to be said about the fear of 'contagion', a Victorian expression which linked disease to poverty. Yet was the British authorities' use of the word 'race' a reference to a determined biological category? Victorian contemporaries had a fluctuating definition of the word 'race', as can be seen in the following excerpt of a Monklands journal: 'there are two distinct races of Irishmen: the Celt and the Saxon, the Roman Catholic and the Protestant, and that the two *races* have always been and are at present antagonistic to each other on everything'.[16] The use of the word 'race' here is ambiguous as its

DOI: 10.1057/9781137329844

meaning swings from a linguistic and racial sense (Celt and Saxon within a same people, the Irish) to a religious logic (Catholic and Protestant). Catherine Hall summarized the Victorian attitude to the word in writing that '[r]ace and nation were used virtually interchangeably for much of the nineteenth century, and "race" could carry a mix of cultural, religious, historical and physical connotations'.[17] Taking into account the variations of the Victorian notion of 'race', Sheridan Gilley has argued against the existence of a positivist racism against the Irish, claiming that Curtis had imported an American vision of society to British society. Similarly, Donald MacRaild has argued that intense prejudice and hostility rather than racism defined the British reception of the Irish in the nineteenth century.[18]

On a local level, the fear of 'non-civilized' Irish subjects also emerged. When looking at the 1851–1921 period, there were certainly times of heightened prejudice, such as the 1850s and 1860s. It would thus seem that the Irish, no matter their denomination, were viewed by the Scots as unquestionably different: their *otherness* set them apart from their hosts.[19] If the Protestant Irish were keen to discard any Irishness that might have hindered their progress in Scotland, the Scots were ready to look upon them as essentially Irish, as a correspondent wrote in the local paper in 1857: '[Irish] Roman Catholics about Coatbridge… are not in a state of the highest civilisation, and that the number of Orangemen or Irish Protestants is also great, and that their civilisation is also at a low ebb'.[20]

The 1860s invectives against the Irish must be analysed in relation to a larger British context. As Catherine Hall has clearly demonstrated, working class agitation, the Fenian scare and the debate surrounding Governor Eyre's handling of Black Jamaicans during the Morant Bay Rebellion (October 1865) reinforced a global British middle class sense of the superiority of the Anglo-Saxon race (defined as white, male, dominant and authoritative).[21] In that context, middle class fears of Irish 'depravity' were expressed locally, both by urban élites and town authorities.

This negative Scottish perception was confirmed in an 1872 Monklands newspaper article: 'But yet, it must be admitted that in the nature and constitution of certain classes of the Irish – without reference to creed, alike Protestant and Catholic – there seems to be something decidedly peculiar'.[22] Were the 'prejudice' mentioned by the Belfast writer or the 'peculiar' otherness of Irish people signs of an anti-Irish racism? The partisans of a racialized perspective on the Irish in Britain have emphasized

DOI: 10.1057/9781137329844

the Irish nationalist stance on the existence of a separate 'race'. Was the 'imagined' Gaelic race not a political argument invented by nineteenth-century Irish nationalists? In the nationalist mythology, the Irish were supposed to be, as a race, direct descendents from the Gaels who had settled on the isle between the sixth and the fifth centuries BC. Also, the English or the Scots used the word 'race' to sometimes ascribe certain physiological and psychological characteristics to the Irish *Paddy*. Yet the heart of the controversy on Anglo-saxon racism towards the Irish Celts is not about whether élite and popular racist attitudes, based on the diffusion of pseudoscientific Victorian research on racial hierarchies, existed. It is rather about how much this racism influenced all political and social attitudes towards the Irish migrants. From a local Scottish perspective, however, it would be difficult to argue that a racialized vision of the Irish was what commanded local responses to the sons of Erin. The racial focus might be an interesting tool of analysis in certain Scoto-Irish political and social fights, but it most certainly does not account for the immense spectrum of Scottish prejudice against the Irish.

Sectarianism redefined

More than racism, as regards attitudes to the Irish diaspora in Scotland, the term 'sectarianism' seems best suited to define Scottish visions of the Irish. Sectarianism can be defined as a complex blend of political, social and religious prejudice. Although historians and sociologists still debate the extent and the duration of sectarianism in Scotland, there is no denial that sectarian attitudes persisted throughout the Victorian and Edwardian eras.[23]

Surprisingly, as T.M. Devine has argued, sectarianism in Scotland has been 'rarely defined and often misunderstood'.[24] Etymologically, the word relates to 'the hostility between different churches or "sects" which has manifested itself in the wider arena of social and political conflict'.[25] The Victorian preferred version was the word 'bigotry' which simply indicated religious antagonism between Protestants and Roman Catholics. Yet what remains unclear is whether sectarianism or rejection of their Catholic counterparts (as they stood as a religious minority in Presbyterian Scotland) was mostly practised by Scots or by Irish Protestants. Second, what kind of attitudes could be classified as being sectarian? From the 'undue favouring of, a particular denomination'

DOI: 10.1057/9781137329844

(as defined by the *Oxford English Dictionary)* in terms of employment or residence to overt violence displayed by one sect against a different denomination, sectarianism took on multiple forms. Effectively, religious prejudice could be displayed in sermons on both sides by clergymen or it could turn into street violence. In that case, the debate was in no sense theological, it rather mingled religious and ethnic antagonisms. Therefore, can one distinguish between 'soft' sectarianism' or 'violent' sectarianism or would it amount to confusing theory (religious antagonism) with its practices?

Another delicate issue relates to the protagonists of sectarianism. It remains difficult to assess whether sectarian tension opposed Irish Catholics and Scottish Protestants or if it was an 'imported Irish' quarrel.[26] Furthermore the gap existing between the reality of sectarianism and its manifestations and the perceptions of religious discrimination must be closely examined. There were also 'official' forms of sectarianism or at least which were perceived as such by Irish Catholics – as the latter sometimes felt that the judicial system was partial to (Irish) Protestants. The *Free Press* expressed that feeling in 1852 when describing the Greenock local authorities: 'How long will the magistrates of Greenock prostitute the ends of justice? One law for the Catholics and another law for the Protestants.'[27] Yet another type of 'whiggish' discourse on the progression of the Irish Catholic community was underway in the late nineteenth century, which tended to tone down the reality or the effects of sectarianism.[28]

'Kick the Pope!' Scotsmen and anti-Catholicism

Anti-Catholicism in mid-Victorian Scotland manifested itself in two main ways: first, in sermons and conferences given by Presbyterian ministers and second, in street preaching. The restoration of the Catholic hierarchy in England in 1851 provoked a surge of Scottish anti-Catholic feeling, and in the 1850s anti-Papist sermons became frequent in Dissenting Presbyterian churches. For example, in 1852, parishioners assembled in Greenock's Free Middle Church to attend a lecture organized by the Greenock Protestant Defence Association. The key speaker, Rev. Rogerson Cooter, vividly depicted his experience in Ireland: '[the Catholics were] crawling round holy wells in order to cleanse them from their sins... He could not look back without shuddering, on the

DOI: 10.1057/9781137329844

long night of darkness which he passed, as a Protestant minister placed amongst a dense Roman Catholic population.'[29] Darkness, obscurantism, superstition were familiar features attributed to Catholic practices. Yet the Catholic clergy did respond to various Protestant pulpit attacks. For instance, in 1851, Father Danaher of Greenock explained that: 'Assertions had been made by a respectable Protestant clergyman of this town to the effect that Catholicity lowered the scale of morality wherever it prevailed. In answering this charge [he] was under the necessity of comparing the moral statistics of Protestants and Catholic countries.'[30] This bears testimony to the fact that Irish Catholics were not always defenceless victims of sectarian attacks. Priests, for instance, did frequently retaliate. Some Catholics were even ready to surf on the Disruption wave and mock Protestant schisms. In Airdrie, the schoolmaster James McAuley engaged in a war of words with Rev. Jackson, a Free Kirk minister, and emphasized the strength of a united faith against the weakness of divided Presbyterianism: 'but as your faith changes with every wind and blast of doctrine, you would find it very difficult to make an obstinate Papist believe that Established Churchism is the true faith one year, and Free Churchism the only saving faith the next.'[31] The Dissenters were effectively very active in the struggle against papal revival: in 1856, Dr Cahill delivered a lecture during a conference organized by Free Church members of the Reformation Society on 'the alarming progress of Popery' in Airdrie.[32] Effectively, the growth and progress of Catholicism occurred at a time when Scottish Protestant churches were divided – so proclaimed Catholic unity was not well received in the face of Presbyterian partition.

Street preaching against Catholics could lead to physical violence. For example, the actions of John Sayers Orr, a.k.a. the 'Angel Gabriel', in Greenock resulted in several severe fights in the early 1850s. Orr was described by Handley as 'an illiterate half-wit whose legal name was John Sayers Orr but who preferred to call himself the "Angel Gabriel". He dressed for the part, on the model of pious woodcuts.'[33] In July 1851, Orr assembled many thousand people during several days on the Greenock docks. On the 14th of July, he led the mob down the streets to St Mary's church, which had its windows smashed by stones. The irate mob went on to beat up some Catholic inhabitants and ransack their houses. As a result, the burgh authorities grew frightened and a Highland regiment was stationed in the town to maintain order.[34] As Father Michael Condon later wrote in his diaries, the main protagonists were local 'artisans'.[35] At

DOI: 10.1057/9781137329844

the time, the mob had been incited to violence by Orr's sermons and also by the circulation of a short-lived Catholic local paper *The Mirror* (which ran from January to July 1851) launched by Father James Danaher. Similar events took place in 1855, when the Catholic church and presbytery in Greenock were attacked by an unruly throng, whose ringleaders were tried at the Edinburgh High Court several months later.[36] From the testimonies collected, it emerges that Orr's anti-Catholicism was combined with populism (against local elites) and chauvinism (he called himself a 'Briton' versus the Irish 'Greeks, and Mickes and Maliesians').[37] The court archives confirm Condon's remark on the 1851 ringleaders, with four Scottish apprentice carpenters (aged 15 to 20) being indicted, amongst whom one was a Gaelic-speaking Highlander. These incidents show that there was a strong 'anti-Establishment' element in those demonstrations. The street preachers mentioned appeared to be waging a war against papal tyranny and furthermore against any type of excessive form of civil authority. In line with such position, it might be added that the Roman Catholics could appear to be 'victims' of the alleged tyrannical power of the papacy and priesthood. The initial attacks were less directed at Catholic Irish than they were at a supposedly vicious Roman hegemony, for Protestants were prompt to react to what they viewed as Papal interference. Thus, over half a century later, when the *Ne Temere* decree (1907) which waged a war against mixed marriages was enforced, some Scotsmen felt that 'they had no want of Christian feelings towards Roman Catholics as individuals... Their quarrel was with the Papal power [which had] no right to interfere with the civil liberties of other people'.[38] From 1851 onwards, the instigators of street religious upheavals claimed to preserve what they thought was a Scottish Covenanting tradition of resistance to unjust powers.

Although preacher-led riots were less frequent during the late Victorian era, on certain occasions this type of religious tension could resurface. Orr found a successor, albeit not as charismatic, in the person of Gavazzi, an Italian ex-priest who toured Scotland on an anti-popery campaign in the 1870s.[39] Other preachers such as Jacob Primmer organized conventicles throughout the West of Scotland in the late 1890s.[40] The Catholics were not the only targets of Primmer's ire – in a 1895 Greenock meeting, he attacked the Kirk whom he found too 'Roman' to his taste.[41] This new generation of anti-ritualistic street preachers were condemned by the local liberal press: 'hardly anybody now takes Jacob altogether seriously... to deliberately menace the peace of the community and

DOI: 10.1057/9781137329844

exasperate the religious feelings of any section of it is not calculated to gain the approbation of intelligent people'.[42] No serious riot was sparked by such gatherings – nevertheless, in March 1899, a respectable Irish Catholic of Greenock, the secretary of the local Trades Council, James Slaven, was arrested following his attack on Ruthgen, an ex-priest on a preaching tour. Slaven was leniently dealt with by Sheriff Begg who sentenced him to a fine and no imprisonment.[43]

Pub (sub)culture?

In his study of the Irishmen in Cumbria, Donald MacRaild emphasized how 'the public house was at the heart of working-class community networks, and the local Irish Catholics, whose reputation for drink was well established, cannot be seen as blameless when violence erupted'.[44] Quarrels between Scots and Irish also manifested themselves in the form of drunken brawls or fighting at the workplace. This everyday violence was condemned by local elites. In 1852 Greenock, the press reported that:

> For some time back the workmen of the town have been in the habit of collecting in mobs in certain localities and beating every Catholic who come in their way... They usually detach themselves in groups of from twenty to fifty; and when any one is discovered whom they suppose to be a Catholic, three or four approach him and urge him to say 'to hell with the Pope'. Non compliance is the signal for an immediate onslaught.[45]

However, it remains difficult to ascertain whether these street clashes occurred amongst Irishmen or whether Scotsmen took an active part in them. In July 1864, a group of Airdrie Irishmen refused to leave a public-house at closing time. The police was called in and managed to throw out the recalcitrant Irish. Yet, after the incident, a group of 40 Scots attacked the Irish party waging war cries such as 'Kill the Irish!'. The local press deplored 'one of those collisions between the Scottish and Irish inhabitants which are becoming so unhappily prevalent both here and at other places'.[46] Even if Scotsmen were involved, it is hard to clearly dissociate Scotch-Irish brawls from internal Irish disputes, as the Scottish local press was usually eager to deplore this 'importation' of Irish quarrels on Caledonian soil. For instance, the fights that took place during 12th of July demonstrations were ascribed to 'Orange and Green' disputes.

DOI: 10.1057/9781137329844

Orange Order and urban disorder

A closer look at the infamous 'Orange and Green' conflicts must start out with a study of Orangeism in the West of Scotland – 'a fraternity founded in the North of Ireland in 1795 whose constitution commits its members to the Defence of Protestantism and the British Crown'.[47] From the 1850s, the growth of the Orange Order in the West of Scotland was undeniable: in Greenock, there were 16 lodges in 1897 within the No. 3 and No. 4 Districts.[48] In the Monklands, the Order was prosperous with five lodges in Airdrie in 1875 and 12 lodges in Coatbridge by the mid-1880s.[49] In addition, the Orangemen erected halls in the Monklands, thus acquiring an urban visibility – in Airdrie the building was of Roman inspiration, with 'an ornamental panel of stone...in which will be carved in *bas-relief* a large equestrian statue of King William'.[50] In Coatbridge, a meeting place allowing for 350 people to assemble was edified in Crichton Street in 1892.[51]

Until the 1870s 'the rough culture of Orangeism... threatened to drag Protestant as well as Catholic Irish under this blanket of racially-inspired opprobrium'.[52] Yet the Order could not be narrowed down to violence and marching, as it was also a 'centre of sociability and camaraderie'.[53] While the Orange Order was developing in the three towns, Orangemen were clearly in search of a specific image, in order to thwart the Scottish elites' chiefly negative perception of Williamite lodges. The Order defined itself as a highly respectable Masonic Order defending 'union among all Protestants, attachment to the Bible and the house of God, and to a Protestant throne and Constitution'.[54] However, the Orangemen's first commandment, that of religious 'attachment' was not often obeyed as Protestant ministers repeatedly insisted on their lack of religious practice. For example, William Harris Winter, a Coatbridge Irish Episcopalian minister, who was District Grand Chaplain, lectured his brethren in 1896 on their abandon: 'unless they attended church regularly and read their Bibles, they were not following out the rules of the Orange lodge'.[55] Regarding loyalty, Orange devotion to the Crown was occasionally mocked by their Scottish contemporaries: a Greenock journalist thus wrote in 1900 that 'times have changed since those devoted loyalists threatened to kick the Queen's crown into the Boyne', alluding to the Order's fight against the disestablishment of the Church of Ireland in the late 1860s.[56] The Greenock District Lodge Grand Master answered back: 'It is not honourable on your part to tarnish the loyalty

DOI: 10.1057/9781137329844

of the Institution, when we can count our numbers by the thousands, and at least two distinguished generals, who are fighting in support of Her Majesty's arms in South Africa.'[57] The Scottish middle classes' attitude towards Orangeism was ambivalent: when Boyne demonstrations turned into violent clashes, the Orangemen were condemned as Irish war fighters; yet, the Orangemen's pursuit of British respectability was also acknowledged by Scottish elites. Accordingly, when 12th of July demonstrations were about to take place, the local press would sometimes issue warnings: 'We are threatened with an Orange invasion or... war dance. The victory that is commemorated on that day is almost purely of Irish significance.'[58]

In Scotland, the membership of the Order was essentially of Irish Protestant origin.[59] Thus the quarrels which occurred during 12th July parades were interpreted by Scottish public opinion as Irish fights. In an attempt to prevent street disorder, parading was banned in many Lanarkshire towns throughout the 1850s. However, reactions to Orange demonstrations varied according to local circumstances. For example, the Greenock Town council had an ambivalent attitude towards Orange demonstrators. In 1852, the municipal authorities allowed an Orange march and orchestra to take place because councillors felt that 'they should encourage the Protestant people rather than keep them down'.[60]

Notwithstanding, some Scotsmen took part in the Irish–Protestant led Orange movement and its leaders were confident that Scotland would consider the Order as a respectable institution. As William Johnstone, an Irish MP, declared before a Greenock reunion of Orangemen in 1874:

> Those days had gone by and that it was not necessary to tell intelligent Scotsmen that Orangemen were the lineal descendants and rightful successors of those who honoured and revered the names of John Knox, John Calvin and Martin Luther – (cheers) – that they were not an Irish faction.[61]

As the Reverend Paterson, a Kirk of Scotland minister declared before a Coatbridge Orange reunion, the Order was opened to others than the Irish, since 'a person of any nationality could join it'.[62]

From the early 1870s to the late 1890s, violent clashes between Protestants and Catholics became less recurrent. The local press still reported on small fights, when their participants were tried before the Burgh police court. The great majority of these fighters were Irish or of Irish origin. Even though the papers did not, as a rule, mention the

DOI: 10.1057/9781137329844

partakers' nationality, when the terms 'party fights' or 'party row' were used, one just had to 'read the names and summonses of those who have been before the authorities for rioting [to] be able to form an opinion of their nationality'.[63] Street brawls could occur after one party had provoked the other. In 1880 a group of Irish Catholic youngsters walked the streets of Gartsherrie armed with sticks shouting: 'To h – – with Billy!' and 'Hourrah for Dan!'.[64] In 1888, two Irishwomen from Greenock were arrested for having breached the peace because they had been 'dancing a bit Irish jig and singing a bit Orange song'.[65]

Nevertheless, the type of incidents cited above did not result in severe rioting and seemed to become less frequent in the late Victorian period. In this global 'appeasement' context, one last major urban riot took place in Coatbridge in the summer of 1883 before it spread to Airdrie and Greenock. The day after the 12th of July demonstration in Coatbridge, which had assembled 14,000 Orangemen, several fights occurred in the Rosehall area – however, the rapid intervention of the police that led to the apprehending of 70 people between July 13th and 11th August prevented further brawls.[66] The next source of agitation was the Irish nationalist parade on Saturday August 18 whereby 3,000 Irishmen demonstrated in the streets of Coatbridge.[67] Fighting between demonstrators and Orangemen started over the week-end, and by Monday the 20th, members of the rival factions were walking in town, armed with spikes. After a series of brawls had taken place, Sheriff Clark read the Riot Act on the steps of the Whitelaw Fountain and the ringleaders were arrested and tried at the Airdrie High Court Session. They were severely punished: as even though no one had been killed during the uprisings, they were still sentenced to several years of imprisonment.[68] The Orange lodge masters departed from their early attitude, in that they strongly denied their involvement in the risings. In Coatbridge, the Orange executive instructed Professor Macklin to inquire into the so-called participation of Orangemen, and the former stated that the lodges were clearly above suspicion (whereas Sheriff Clark insisted on the involvement of both 'Catholics and Orangemen').[69]

In Greenock, where similar disturbances took place in August 1883, the Orange District master, Alexander Stell, sent an official letter to the local press where he certified that:

> We, the representatives of the Orangemen of Greenock in District Lodge assembled, hereby beg to repudiate all knowledge or connection with the party disturbance at present existing in town, and denounce such rioting in

DOI: 10.1057/9781137329844

the strongest terms as most disgraceful. We also pledge ourselves to assist the authorities in every lawful way to prevent all such riots or disturbances, and any of our Order guilty of participating in such will be dealt with for violation of our laws of constitution.[70]

The gradual disappearance of serious rioting up until the 1920s needs to be accounted for. Two major factors can clarify this pacification of religious and social tensions: first, the severe repression of all party incidents after 1883 seemed to have acted as a deterrent. Following the great 1883 Coatbridge riot, the municipal and police authorities were prompt to react to any sign of a disturbance. During the summer of 1884, in August, a party of Orange musicians fought with Irish Catholics in Airdrie.[71] Following this event, community leaders including priests (on the Irish Catholic side) were fast to intervene when 'in the various Roman Catholic chapels in the district last Sunday, the officiating clergymen addressed their congregations after mass, and impressed on them the advisability of refraining from any appearance of dissent'.[72] For his part, Sheriff Mair wrote to all local Orange lodges to demand that they let a scheduled Irish nationalist demonstration take place without disturbance.[73] The Monkland magistrates let no presumed 'rioter' go unpunished: in October 1885, a stone-throwing boy, Samuel Hill, aged 12, was condemned to be flogged for having thrown stones at a party of Catholic schoolboys (in ordinary circumstances, punishment for bullying was left to schoolmasters).[74] Local citizens even complained to national authorities down in London of the strictness of municipal rule: in 1885, Scotsmen and Orangemen wrote to the Home Secretary to complain of the 60-day sentence given by local magistrates to the members of the Rosehall Flute and Protestant Band accused of having played ultra-protestant tunes and songs.[75]

Secondly, street violence seemed to lessen because discontents were partly channelled by the growing political and nationalist organizations. On both the Catholic and Protestant Irish sides, friendly socio-political societies were developing.[76] In 1891, The Orange Amalgamated District Friendly Society was opened to Monkland Orangemen.[77] The membership was restricted to an 'active member of some Orange lodge' of 'good moral character'.[78] The quest for respectability was very strong in the Orange organizations, as demonstrated by the lodges' masters reactions during the 1883 riots, whereby the latter denied Orange partaking in what they considered as 'disgraceful' brawls. On the whole, 12th of July sectarian incidents were extremely rare, because of the Order's careful

DOI: 10.1057/9781137329844

preparation and of police arrangements. Accordingly, in 1908, the District Master of the L.O.L. No. 1 (Airdrie) wrote to the Chief Constable:

> thanking you on behalf of the whole Orange Brotherhood of this district for your courtesy, and for the excellent arrangements you made and carried out for the comfort and convenience of the brethren on the occasion of the 12th of July celebrations this year… It is the aim and hope of all the office-bearers of the Orange brotherhood in this district to be regarded as orderly and law-abiding citizens.[79]

Nevertheless, Scottish anti-Orangeism could still occasionally resurface during the Edwardian era, as evidenced in the Greenock press in 1906: 'Orangemen are neither Ulster nor Scot, but a hybrid breed, who inherit all the sins and none of the virtues of both the Scottish and Irish.'[80] Furthermore, the Order's secret initiation was mocked: 'It would be worth considering whether a man belonging to a secret society having signs, grips, and passwords, and sworn to give favour and preference to brother members on all occasions is really fitted to fill a public office.'[81]

Towards an end to sectarian attitudes?

At first glance, it would appear as if the Edwardian era was a time when Irish Catholics felt that Scottish antagonism was on the wane. For instance, in May 1903, the Glasgow Archdiocese celebrated the 25th anniversary of the Catholic hierarchy's restoration. The general atmosphere was optimistic,[82] as reflected in the *Catholic Directory*:

> We no longer suffer from active persecution or from the open and general display of intolerance. It is true that we have yet to complain of a certain amount of misrepresentation and misunderstanding on the part of non-Catholics; that even in this matter of 'toleration' it is sometimes expected that we should be tolerant to the extent of submitting without protest to statements which we know to be unfair and misleading. But, judging from what has already happened, we may confidently expect that our difficulties will diminish, while our resources and influence will continue to increase… We have, now at least, no barrier to our progress.[83]

The Church's progressive integration into the Scottish religious landscape was visible, both in a material and symbolic way. From an urban perspective, 'with the rise and progress of Coatbridge the Roman Catholics of the district have also helped considerably to beautify the town from an architectural

DOI: 10.1057/9781137329844

point of view', stated the *Coatbridge Express* in 1903.[84] As concerns the Catholic clergy, events involving the priesthood seemed to be reported in a similar manner as matters that concerned local Protestant ministers. Furthermore, town officials attended major Catholic events such as burials or anniversaries. In 1901, Father Michael Condon, the former priest of Saint Lawrence's (he had left in 1885) was congratulated by Greenock town councillors for his nomination as a canon of the Glasgow chapter. In Coatbridge, in 1902, two Scottish magistrates attended the inauguration of an altar dedicated to the late Father Michael O'Keeffe, of Saint Patrick's.[85]

Yet this better acceptance of Catholic institutions, as they became part of the Scots' urban heritage, did not wholly put an end to all sectarian attitudes. Rejection of the Irish on account of their nationality and/or their religion could still be manifested at official levels. Several instances of public disapproval of Irish behaviour occurred during the Edwardian period. Reprobation of the desecration of the Sabbath repose was brought forward in 1902 by Coatdyke denizens who complained of Irishmen playing cards on a Sunday: 'we are being dragged down to the lowest depths of degradation by those pests that infest our land. It might do well in the wilds of Donegal.'[86] Scottish members of municipal authorities could also be severe towards newly arrived Irish migrants who did not blend in as well as members of the older generations. In 1909, town councillor David in Coatbridge told off two Irish navvies in the Burgh Court: 'A lot of you Irishmen think you have a right to come here and disgrace the town. You will get the town a bad character. You think you have a right to fight and quarrel when you like.'[87]

As regards religious quarrels, in spite of the Catholic Church's official optimistic version of integration in the Scottish landscape, some Irish Catholics still felt they had to justify their rights as British subjects. In 1908, John McGovern, the headmaster of Saint Patrick school (Coatbridge), sent a letter to the local press where he reminded his Scottish counterparts that the Irish Catholics were not 'the sworn subjects of a foreign power... In temporal matters our allegiance is due to the King... and every child who goes through a Catholic school has to learn it in his catechism.'[88]

Self-visions of Irishness in the Edwardian era

At the turn of the century, as Irish political organization grew in Scotland, what it meant to be Irish was increasingly defined by local nationalist

DOI: 10.1057/9781137329844

leaders. Irish political activists became more assertive as regards their own identity and the ways in which they imposed it on their country-men. In January 1901, a quarrel divided the members of the Airdrie local United Irish League, when John Power, the secretary, resigned after fighting with its president over the invitation of a local Trade Unionist, Chisholm Robertson.[89] The two Leaguers argued over the purpose of the meeting, and Power ended the debate by stating that Robertson was 'a better Irishman than any of the men who attacked him after his address to this branch'.[90] Hanratty answered back that '...Mr. Roberston never laid claim to being an Irishman, but has always held that although he was a Catholic in religion he is a Scotchman in nationality'.[91]

This statement epitomized the Irish identity issue in post-Victorian Scotland, with its ambiguous mingling of religious and national features. By saying that 'although a Catholic' he was a Scotchman, Robertson (quoted by Hanratty) countered the systematic assumption that every Catholic should be Irish. However, Power went on arguing in favour of Robertson' Irishness, by explaining that the latter's father was Scottish (hence his name) yet a Nationalist and that his mother was a Catholic Irish. Hanratty ended up attacking Power's surname, stating that he was known as 'Pyers' – to which Power replied: 'Those who are acquainted with Irish history shall have no difficulty in identifying my name as Irish'.[92] This debate encapsulated the complexity of being Irish – an identity which was neither hereditary, nor political nor religious. It also echoed tensions surrounding the preservation of an identity which could potentially be toned down by second and third generation Irish. The great rallies organized in Glasgow, Greenock and Coatbridge in the 1900s, which gathered together natives of various Irish counties, could be thus interpreted as gestures of defence against the loss of Irishness.[93] For instance, when the natives of County Donegal assembled in Greenock, in 1907, their purpose was to 'stimulate and sustain the interest which every true Irishman should take in the affairs of his country and to keep alive the views and ideals ... they were liable to lose in an alien atmosphere'.[94] The efficiency of these meetings in terms of keeping Irishness alive was doubtful. One 'disgusted Donegal man', who had attended the Greenock meeting, mentioned above, wrote to the local press stating that nobody was able to sing past the first verse of *God Save Ireland*.[95]

In addition, the incoming of new migrants, both Italian and Lithuanian, in the late nineteenth and early twentieth century, contrib-uted towards the change of the Scottish perception of the Irish. In 1903, a

DOI: 10.1057/9781137329844

Coatbridge Express leader expressed hostile feelings towards Lithuanians by stating that 'The Pole in crime is becoming as serious a factor in social life… The Pole's reckless brutality, amounting, occasionally, to barbarous savagery'.[96]

Moreover, 'Poles' (that is how Scots named Lithuanians) had to resort to methods which the Irish never had had to use – for instance, they would transform their surname into a Scottish-sounding surname, so as to avoid patent rejection. However, the story of a young Lithuanian girl who was brought to the Coatbridge Burgh Court demonstrated that choosing a surname was no easy task. The press report mocked the poor girl, for she bore 'the Irish name of Flanigan'![97] How ironical to select an Irish name in hoping that it would soothe Scottish burgh authorities! The Lithuanians' precarious situation contrasted with the Irish communities' relative stability in early twentieth century, for when a Pole (Peter Mitchell) was arrested in 1906 Coatbridge and condemned on a charge of violence, the Burgh Procurator declared that: 'this man was an alien… this was a case in which the Aliens' Act should be brought back into operation, and that accused should in terms of that Act be sent back to Poland as an undesirable'.[98]

Conclusion

The Irishness of Catholic and Protestant migrants was constructed in various ways, in which Scottish perceptions were as important as 'Orange' and 'Green' political agendas. Irish identities in Airdrie, Coatbridge and Greenock were sometimes toned down or, on the contrary, loudly publicly proclaimed on streets and in great gatherings. The specificity of the Scottish experience demonstrates how religion rather than race explained Scottish attitudes towards the Irish. The influence of Liberalism in Scottish Western towns also helped Scottish contemporaries in some cases better to accept the case for demonstrations of Irish nationalism.

This exploration of sectarianism in Western Scottish towns has demonstrated that it was a multifarious phenomenon, implemented by different sections of the Catholic and Protestant communities. It could refer to a Scots Protestant/Irish Catholic antagonism which had religious and theological bases (as seen with the no-popery sermons) or, most frequently, to an interethnic conflict opposing Irish Protestants and Irish

DOI: 10.1057/9781137329844

Catholics. As the nineteenth century drew to a close, the most visible forms of sectarianism such as 'Green-Orange' street fights, were declining. In many aspects, the 1910s was a period when religious and ethnic antagonism was less a street-level fight and more an associational and political combat.[99]

Notes

1   C. Camilleri (1990) 'Identité et gestion de la disparité culturelle: essai d'une typologie' in C. Camilleri (ed.) *Stratégies identitaires* (Paris: PUF), p. 86.
2   See S. Gilley (1978) 'English Attitudes to the Irish in England, 1780–1900' in C. Holmes (ed.) *Immigrants and Minorities in British Society* (London: Allen and Unwin), pp. 81–110.
3   L. Colley (1992) 'Britishness and Otherness: An Argument', *Journal of British Studies*, 31, pp. 309–29.
4   L. Colley (1992) 'Britishness and Otherness', p. 325.
5   L. Colley does not really tackle the thorny issue of Irishness within Britishness: see also P. O'Sullivan (ed.) (1996) *The Irish World Wide: History, Heritage, Identity. Vol. V: Religion and Identity* (London: Leicester University Press), p. 9.
6   G. Walker (1991) 'The Protestant Irish in Scotland' in T. Devine (ed.) *Irish Immigrants and Scottish Society in the Nineteenth and Twentieth Centuries* (Edinburgh: John Donald), pp. 45–6.
7   The 1845 Poor Law allowed for the relief of those who could give proof of a certain number of years of residence in the parish they applied to.
8   *AC*, 21 July 1865.
9   D. MacRaild (1996) '"Principle, Party and Protest": The Language of Victorian Orangeism in the North of England' in S. West (ed.) *The Victorians and Race* (Aldershot: Scholar Press), p. 135. This theory is expressed by D. Akenson (1988) *Small Differences: Irish Catholics and Irish Protestants, 1815–1922: An International Perspective* (Kingston: McGill-Queen's University Press).
10 P. Panayi (1994) *Immigration, Ethnicity and Racism in Britain, 1815–1945* (Manchester: Manchester University Press), p. 76; P. Gleason (1983) 'Identifying Identity: A Semantic History', *The Journal of American History*, 69/4, p. 919.
11 L. P. Curtis (1968) *Anglo-Saxons and Celts – A Study of Anti-Irish Prejudice in Victorian England* (New York: New York University Press); M. J. Hickman (1999) 'Alternative Historiographies of the Irish in Britain: A Critique of the Segregation/Assimilation Model' in R. Swift and S. Gilley (eds) *The Irish in Victorian Britain: The Local Dimension* (Dublin: Dublin Four Court Press), p. 247.

12   As is confirmed by tenants of the revisionist approach to Irish history: see
      G. K. Peatling (2005) 'The Whiteness of Ireland Under and After the Union',
      Journal of British Studies, 44, p. 115: 'racism certainly cannot be reduced to
      chromatism or prejudice based on skin color…'; L. Perry Curtis (2005)
      'Comment: The Return of Revisionism', *Journal of British Studies*, 44, pp.
      134–45.

13   As summarized by G. K. Peatling (2005): 'This is not to suggest that
      no instances of the racialization of the irish occurred or that they were
      insignificant' in 'The Whiteness of Ireland', p. 126.

14   F. Engels (1844), *The Condition of the Working-Class in England in 1844*
      (London: George Allen & Unwin , 1943 ed.), pp. 92–3.

15   PP, *Eight Decennial Census of the Population of Scotland Taken April 3rd 1871 with
      Report*. p. XXXIV.

16   *AC*, 26 October 1867.

17   C. Hall (2012) *Macaulay and Son. Architects of Imperial Britain* (New Haven &
      London: Yale University Press), p. 204.

18   S. Gilley (1978) 'English Attitudes to the Irish'; M. A. G. O'Tuathaigh (1985)
      'The Irish in Nineteenth Century Britain : Problems of Interpretation' in
      R. Swift and S. Gilley (eds) *The Irish in the Victorian City* (London: Croom
      Helm), p. 22.

19   Elaine McFarland has shown the links between Irish immigration and the
      development of the Orange Order in Victorian Scotland: E. McFarland
      (1990) *Protestants First: Orangeism in Nineteenth Century Scotland* (Edinburgh:
      Edinburgh University Press).

20   *AC*, 18 July 1857. Note that Orangemen are equated with Irish Protestants
      here. See also *AC*, 2 November 1867.

21   C. Hall (1993) 'White Visions, Black Lives: The Free Villages of Jamaica',
      History Workshop, 36, pp. 100–32.

22   *AC*, 24 August 1872.

23   Both inside and outside the academic world, the sectarian issue in Scotland
      has been intensely debated during the past decade. From Tom Devine's
      edited collection *Scotland's Shame? Bigotry and Sectarianism in Modern Scotland*
      in 2000 to more recent books and press articles, the question of Scotland's
      sectarian past has been addressed by historians, sociologists and various
      writers. Some researchers have even dismissed it as an exaggerated myth,
      in the sense that it could not be compared with sectarianism in Northern
      Ireland. In a 2011 article published in *The Guardian*, the historian Steve Bruce
      explained that 'when Irish migrants settled in large numbers at the end of the
      19th and start of the 20th century, some Scots objected to what they feared
      was union-bashing cheap labour. Others objected to what they believed
      was a false and dangerous religion'. Steve Bruce, 'Scottish sectarianism?
      Let's Lay this Myth to Rest', 24 April 2011 at http://www.guardian.co.uk/

DOI: 10.1057/9781137329844

commentisfree/belief/2011/apr/24/scotland-sectarianism-research-data, date
accessed 2 March 2012. He further made clear that in terms of workforce,
residence and education, Scotland was never as divided as Northern
Ireland had been. Although the chronology put forward by Steve Bruce
(late nineteenth–early twentieth centuries) should be revised in the sense
that the 'troubles' started in the 1830s, he does make a point in contesting
the too great an importance given by some writers to the role played by
sectarianism in Scottish society. For discussion on sectarianism, see: S.
Bruce, A. Glendinning, I. Paterson, M. Rosie (2004) *Sectarianism in Scotland*
(Edinburgh: Edinburgh University Press).

24   T. M. Devine (2010) 'The End of Disadvantage?' in M.J. Mitchell (ed.), *New
     Perspectives on the Irish in Scotland* (Edinburgh: John Donald) , p. 201.

25   M. Hogan (1984) 'Whatever happened to Australian Sectarianism?', *Journal of
     Religious History*, 13, p. 83.

26   See G. Walker (1991) 'The Protestant Irish', pp. 51–2.

27   *FP*, 13 January 1852.

28   M. O' Cathàin (2010) '"Dying Irish": Eulogizing the Irish in Scotland in
     Glasgow Observer Obituaries', *The Innes Review*, 31, p. 84.

29   *GA*, 9 January 1852.

30   *FP*, 16 August 1851.

31   *FP*, 21 January 1854.

32   *AC*, 27 December 1857.

33   J. E. Handley (1949) *The Irish in Scotland* (Glasgow: John Burns), p. 234.

34   *FP*, 19 July 1851.

35   SCA, WD/5/1: p. 260.

36   NAS, AD/14/55/280: 1855 High Court indictment versus Robert McEwan,
     Neil McPhaill, Malcom Morrison and Lachlan Cameron, for mobbing and
     rioting.

37   NAS, AD/14/55/280: 1855 High Court indictment versus Robert McEwan,
     Neil McPhaill…: William Orr Leitch's testimony.

38   *GT*, 3 May 1911.

39   *AC*, 25 May 1878.

40   *CE*, 10 July 1901 and 9 July 1902.

41   *GT*, 27 July 1895.

42   *CE*, 6 July 1898.

43   *GE*, 15 April 1899.

44   D. MacRaild (1998) *Culture, Conflict and Migration. The Irish in Victorian
     Cumbria* (Liverpool: Liverpool University Press), p. 183.

45   *FP*, 18 December 1852.

46   *AC*, 16 July 1864.

47   On the scarcity of Orange lodge records, see D. MacRaild (2005) *Faith,
     Fraternity and Fighting. The Orange Order and Irish Migrants in Northern*

DOI: 10.1057/9781137329844

England, c. 1850–1920 (Liverpool: Liverpool University Press), pp. 7–13. See also E. Kaufman (2008) 'The Orange Order in Scotland since 1860: A Social Analysis' in M.J. Mitchell (ed.), *New Perspectives*, p. 159.

48   *GA*, 11 July 1890.

49   *AC*, 14 and 26 July 1879.

50   *CE*, 17 June 1891.

51   *CE*, 21 December 1894.

52   D. MacRaild (1999) *Irish Migrants in Modern Britain, 1750–1922* (London: Macmillan Press), p. 131.

53   D. MacRaild (2005) *Faith, Fraternity and Fighting*, p. 3.

54   *GA*, 11 October 1877.

55   *CE*, 8 July 1896.

56   *GT*, 13 July 1900.

57   *GT*, 17 July 1900.

58   *AC*, 5 July 1873.

59   The same pattern is also distinctive of Orangeism in North-East England: see D. MacRaild (2005) *Faith, Fraternity and Fighting*.

60   *FP*, 24 January 1852. On local authorities' authorization of Orange lodges in England, see D. MacRaild (2005) *Faith, Fraternity and Fighting*, pp. 177–78.

61   *GA*, 14 October 1874.

62   *CE*, 25 October 1898.

63   *AC*, 6 October 1883.

64   *AC*, 18 September 1880.

65   *GT*, 7 September 1888.

66   See T. G. Fraser (2000) *The Irish Parading Tradition: Following the Drum (Ethnic and Intercommunity Conflict)*, (Basingstoke: Palgrave Macmillan); *AC*, 11 August 1883.

67   *AC*, 25 August 1883.

68   *AC*, 8 December 1883.

69   *AC*, 8 December 1883.

70   *GA*, 25 August 1883.

71   *AC*, 16 August 1884.

72   *AC*, 16 August 1884.

73   *AC*, 16 August 1884.

74   *AC*, 3 October 1885.

75   *AC*, 23 May 1885 & 27 June 1885.

76   D. MacRaild (2000) 'Crossing Migrant Frontiers: Comparative Reflections on Irish Migrants in Britain and the United States during the Nineteenth Century', in D. MacRaild (ed.) *The Great Famine and Beyond: Irish Migrants in Britain in the Nineteenth and Twentieth Centuries* (Dublin: Irish Academic Press), p. 58.

77   NAS, FS 4/1063: *Rules of the Orange Amalgamated Districts Friendly Society, no. 506, Lanark.*

DOI: 10.1057/9781137329844

78   NAS, FS 4/1063: *Rules of the Orange Amalgamated Districts Friendly Society, no. 506, Lanark.*

79   *AC*, 1 September 1908.

80   *GT*, 30 October 1906.

81   *GT*, 27 October 1906.

82   On the advent of a whiggish discourse on the progress of the Irish nationality in Scotland, see M. Cathàin (2010) "'Dying Irish'".

83   CD, 1904, p. 240.

84   *CE*, 15 February 1905.

85   *CE*, 10 December 1902.

86   *CE,* 27 August 1902.

87   *CL*, 3 April 1909.

88   *AC*, 21 November 1908.

89   *GE*, 1 June 1901.

90   *GE*, 1 June 1901.

91   *GE*, 1 June 1901.

92   *GE*, 29 June 1901.

93   *GE*, 18 January 1902. Father Richard made this statement at a gathering of the County Monaghan natives in Glasgow.

94   *GT*, 27 November 1907.

95   *GT*, 28 November 1907.

96   *CL*, 24 June 1903.

97   *CE*, 22 February 1905.

98   *CE*, 22 August 1906.

99   See M.J. Mitchell (2008) 'Irish Catholics in the West of Scotland in the Nineteenth Century', in M.J. Mitchell (ed.) *New Perspectives*, p. 7.

DOI: 10.1057/9781137329844

3
Irish Catholic Socializing

Abstract: *Chapter 3 first focuses on the rebuilding of the Catholic Church in the three Western towns describing the particular financial and spiritual needs of Irish parishioners. The Scoto-Irish tensions within the Catholic clergy and laity in the 1860s are also revisited. Next, an examination of Irish Catholic sociability is conducted, with a review of the various existing associations. Particular attention is paid to the nationalist tone of certain Catholic societies, along with their varying definition of Irishness to restrict their membership. A sociological analysis of Saint Patrick's Day celebrations and a study on the ways in which those gatherings evolved ends the chapter.*

Vaughan, Geraldine. *The 'Local' Irish in the West of Scotland, 1851–1921*. Basingstoke: Palgrave Macmillan, 2013. DOI: 10.1057/9781137329844.

DOI: 10.1057/9781137329844

As a result of Irish immigration, Catholicism was resurrected in the West of Scotland. This phenomenon had religious, urban, social and political implications. Moreover, this Catholic resurgence occurred when the Established Church in Scotland was undergoing a deep crisis, in the aftermath of the Disruption (1843) and the creation of the Free Church (1847).[1] Yet, the absence of ecclesiastical hierarchy (prior to 1878) meant that Scotland's status was that of a Mission, divided into three Vicariates in 1827 by Pope Leo XII.[2] Measuring the actual impact of the growth of Catholicism in a Presbyterian land is crucial to an understanding of the world vision of Irish catholic immigrants. The nature of the Scottish Roman Catholic Church and how its authorities reacted to the influx of Irish parishioners must be explored. Moreover, Mary Hickman's stance on the denationalization efforts of the Catholic Church in Britain needs to be reassessed in the Scottish context.[3]

Rebuilding a Roman Catholic world

The revival of the Catholic Church in the West of Scotland beginning in the 1840s was connected to the influx of Irish Catholic immigrants, even though some churches had already been (re)built early in the century.[4] In Airdrie, Saint Margaret's church was consecrated in 1839 in Hallcraig Street and could seat 800 parishioners. From 1840, the Airdrie Mission became an independent parish and its first resident clergyman was Daniel Gallagher:

> After some time the new Mission of Airdrie was confided to his care, embracing a large portion of Lanarkshire, the Catholics being chiefly colliers and miners, scattered over a wide district. This was an arduous charge for the young priest, as he frequently had to traverse on foot long miles by night to the bedside of some poor Catholic stricken either by sickness or accident.[5]

In 1848, Saint Margaret's church was enlarged and could seat 1,010 people from amongst 6,000 recorded Catholics (32 per cent of church-goers according to the 1851 Religious Census).[6] Two years later, the church became highly visible as it was equipped with 'the largest [bell] in Airdrie'.[7] In neighbouring Coatbridge, an independent mission was formed in 1845, and the church of Saint Patrick erected in 1848. The town's religious landscape was shaped by the Baird brothers, the local industrial barons,

DOI: 10.1057/9781137329844

who initiated the building of the Gartsherrie (Established) Church in 1839. The Bairds recognized 'the value of organised religion in keeping a certain discipline among the work force'.[8] Accordingly, they also let a plot of land in Main Street to allow the estimated 5,000 Irish Roman Catholics to have their own church built.[9]

In contrast with the Monkland case, the establishment of a Catholic church in Greenock took place in the early nineteenth century. In 1815, Saint Mary's could accommodate 400 – by the 1830s, the Catholic population of Greenock was over 4,000.[10] Yet Catholics represented only 10 per cent of Greenock's church-goers in 1851 and the distribution of the Protestant affiliations revealed the ascendancy of the dissenting churches. In fact, the overwhelming dominance of Free Kirkers and United Presbyterians (78 per cent of church-goers as opposed to 20 per cent in Glasgow) amongst Greenock Protestants may account for many of the brutal reactions against Irish Catholics throughout the mid-Victorian era. Calvinism was strong in the Free Church and hostility towards 'Romanists' was evident in theological debates and lectures. As Callum Brown explains, 'some ministers, particularly from the Calvinist wing of the Free Church, developed links with artisan Protestant defence organisations.'[11]

The building of churches was followed by the development of cemeteries. In November 1858, the clergy had bought a piece of land lying next to Saint Margaret's and consecrated it. However, this attempt was opposed by the local Scots, who petitioned against a graveyard being built in the middle of their town. During the trial that followed, the Irish Catholics explained their need for their coreligionists to be buried in Catholic sacred ground, yet they lost the case and had to establish a cemetery a few miles away, on a piece of land donated by Sir Archibald Gerard of Rochsoles.[12] Notwithstanding the public hygiene reasons put forward by the Scottish opponents to the cemetery, the real grounds for their resistance probably lay in their refusal to see too many Catholic funeral processions in town. As Patrick McGeehan, an Irish Catholic, ironically explained a few years later: 'as some of the inhabitants complained that the graveyard would be too near their homes. I suppose that they feared they might see spirits there which would naturally depress their own spirits.'[13]

However, the creation of a Catholic cemetery was not a great success with the Catholic community, as the plots were expensive and the overall aspect was not very appealing:

DOI: 10.1057/9781137329844

In the first place, the lairs are too dear... and by far higher than the charges made in our Protestant graveyards here. From its present wretched condition it is a laughing stock to the whole Protestant community, the lairs being in a complete zig-zag fashion.[14]

In Greenock the establishment of a Catholic cemetery proved an easier matter – in 1866, Father Michael Condon was granted permission by the Town Council to purchase 300 square meters area of land within the city's graveyard (the stability of the Catholic presence probably accounted for the town authorities' lack of resistance).[15]

Vox Clamantis in Deserto? A divided Catholic Church

Roman Catholicism in the nineteenth century was subject to varying national 'interpretations' – for instance, within the British empire, Hilary Carey wrote that 'while Irish Catholicism was to triumph in much of the English-speaking empire, this was achieved at the expense of English Catholicism in Australia and New Zealand, and was limited by French Catholicism in British North America'.[16] This quote illustrates how national rivalries divided the expanding Catholic Church in the British colonies. The Scottish mission (before 1878) proved no exception. There was certainly a confrontation between the Scottish devotional version, described as 'reserved, unemotional, isolated in a Presbyterian environment, somewhat tinged with a suspicion of Jansenism', and the Irish, who sought 'more frequent communion, rosary, benediction and catechism'.[17] Conflicts between these competing Irish and Scots visions of Catholicism broke out in 1864 in what is often referred to as the 'Free Press quarrel'. Indeed, the clash between the Irish clergy and the Scottish hierarchy was reported, and largely whipped up by the Catholic newspaper *The Glasgow Free Press*. The dispute which opposed Scottish and Irish members of the clergy has been well researched yet tensions between Scottish ministers and their Irish flock have been subject to less scrutiny.

On the clerical level, the Scottish hierarchy (Vicariate) and clergy feared that Irish Catholicism would pervade the Scottish Catholic Church and change the face of Roman Catholicism.[18] How was 'Irish Catholicism' defined by Scots clergymen? There was essentially a political dimension in the divide, for the Scottish hierarchy had trouble in accepting the nationalist stances of some of the Irish clergymen (many

DOI: 10.1057/9781137329844

had been trained at All Hallows seminary, a hotbed of nationalism in the eyes of certain members of the hierarchy).[19] In that sense, Alexander Smith, the Vicariate Coadjutor, noted in reference to Coatbridge in 1858: 'all well – still the deep, deep nationality'.[20]

On the Irish side, two priests took the lead in the fight against the Scottish hierarchy and clergy: Father Michael O'Keeffe of Coatbridge, chairman of the 22 Irish 'rebel' priests, and Michael Condon of Greenock (Saint Lawrence). The latter sent in May 1864 a list of resolutions to Cardinal Barnabò, prefect of Propaganda Fide, complaining that the Irish priesthood was never consulted, especially on questions of financial administration.[21] The committee representing 'the Catholic Clergy of the Western District of Scotland' stated that it spoke in the name of 'its priests as of the faithful, who Irish by birth or parentage, constitute more than nineteen twentieths of the whole Catholic laity'. The spirit of the various resolutions was summarized by John Murdoch, Apostolic Vicar at the time: 'The second charge is of undisguised partiality to Scotch, and unconcealed neglect and unjust treatment of Irish priests; and finally, a deep-rooted prejudice and bitter antipathy to the flock... solely on account of their country and race'.[22] The *Free Press*, launched in 1851, was instrumental in waging a war against the 'Hielan clique' of Scottish priests. The paper called for the advent of an Irish hierarchy in Scotland as early as 1863. The crisis was such that Archbishop Manning visited the Western Vicariate in October 1867 – in 1869, Charles Eyre, an Englishman, was appointed Apostolic Administrator of the Western Vicariate (he became Archbishop in 1878). Furthermore, the *Free Press* was condemned by Rome in January 1868 on the grounds that it had '... excite[d] hatred among the different nationalities of which Catholicity is amongst us composed'.[23]

Such condemnation proved effective as the *Free Press* ceased publication in February 1868. Thus the Irish-Scotch crisis of the mid-1860s did seem to be a great war waged by infuriated protagonists, but just how many people were actually involved in the conflict? It would appear that only half of the Irish clergy adhered to the group of the 22 radical Irish priests and that the 'Hielan clique' represented just over 60 per cent of the Scottish clergy in the Western Vicariate. The main actors on the Irish side – amongst whom Harry Keane, the *Free Press* editor, Fathers Michael Condon and Michael O'Keeffe – were few in number and they remained stationed in the Western Vicariate after the crisis and developed pacific relationships with the local Scottish clergy. Thus, the fact that the crisis lasted over a short

DOI: 10.1057/9781137329844

period of time (from 1864 to 1868) and ceased after the dismantlement of the *Free Press* and the nomination of Bishop Grey demonstrated that what occurred could be described at best as an adjustment phase rather than a deep-rooted conflict between Scots and Irish clergymen.

Yet tensions, even if they were short-lived, did not solely oppose members of the clergy. At times, there were also 'national' tensions between Scottish priests and their Irish flock. Some Irish nationalists were worried that the native priests would destroy all political aspirations. For example, Charles Muldoon, an Irishman, wrote to Father Michael Condon of Greenock, who was one of the 22 'rebel' Irish priests, in 1868: 'From my recollection of the disposition of the Scotch portion of the Clergy to denationalize the Irish.'[24] In Airdrie, The 'Duncan McNab' affair clearly epitomized the difficulties that could arise between the two nationalities. Duncan McNab was Saint Margaret's vicar in the 1860s and 'was not liked by his flock. He was very stern and frowned upon anything he regarded as frivolous.'[25] In 1862, McNab gave a lecture in Bathgate, a neighbouring village, on Saint Patrick's day, during which he stated that:

> If the Irish were blasphemous and objects of ridicule, who made them so?... If they were a thieving and lying race, suspicion has made them so... They may be liars – lying was the vice of all people oppressed... If they were ignorant, Government was to blame in preventing them from getting up schools in Ireland.[26]

This speech angered his Irish parishioners. McNab defended himself, stating: 'I mentioned blasphemy, ignorance, fighting, thieving, and lying as vices which I had heard ascribed to them. But I never said the allegation was true.'[27] The *Free Press* heated up the 'Airdrie scandal' and a series of letters were published by Scottish clergymen and 'outraged' Irishmen. The underlying conflict was political – McNab thus wrote that: 'I like patriotism; but I cannot venerate nationality as a demigod.'[28]

As regards Irish clergymen and their parishioners, there could also be tense relationships, although many Irish nationalists were prompt to advertise the harmony between the two parties. This was the case with Charles Muldoon, who compared the Scottish situation with that of the rest of the Irish diaspora in 1865:

> I believe that Irishmen never cherish the faith with the same zeal under foreign priests, as when they have Irish priests to sympathise with their struggles and their wants. This is observable in America as well as in Scotland and even in Canada it prevails and to a slight degree in England.[29]

DOI: 10.1057/9781137329844

The *Free Press* further argued that: 'the love of the Irishman for his priest increases in intensity the longer and farther he is removed from his native home'.[30] Yet tensions between the Irish priests and their flocks arose from time to time. In Coatbridge, opposition to the Limerick clergyman, Michael O'Keeffe, for political reasons, led one of the leading parishioners, Hugh O'Hear, to withdraw his children from the Catholic school. O'Keeffe wrote to the Vicariate in 1862: 'I have every reason to complain of Hugh O'Hear who is sending his children to the Protestant school' – furthermore, the latter started going to mass at Airdrie to avoid the Irish priest.[31]

Catholic friendly societies

The Catholic Church aimed at developing faith-based parochial activities.[32] Since numerous Scottish friendly societies barred Catholics from becoming members, the Church was able to create a parallel associational network. Indeed, Scottish lodges such as the *Airdrie Greenhouse Lodge of Free Gardeners* in the Monklands (created in 1812) agreed in 1854 'not to admit any Roman Catholics, Ribbonmen or Orangemen, so that they may not be chargeable in any way as encouraging the above parties to exhibit their party feuds to the danger of the public peace'.[33] Interestingly, both Protestant and Catholic Irishmen were excluded from the lodge. Nevertheless, certain Irish friendly societies were formed outside the Catholic clergy's control. In 1844, the *Airdrie Hibernian Society* was launched by a group of local Irishmen, who endeavoured to provide for Irish miners:

> In the many public works around Airdrie great numbers of Irishmen are employed and many, with their families, are often plunged into a state of destitution from one or other of the above causes and thrown upon the world, amongst strangers, to pick up a precarious subsistence.[34]

Membership rules were applicable to male adults aged between 20 and 42 who must be 'of good moral character, in good health and recommended by two or more members of the Society'.[35] The entry fee was 5 shillings and the annual payments represented 10 shillings (the average weekly salary for working men varied between 12 and 22 shillings); funerals were paid for by the societies and '[e]ach member within the officer's bound of warning (3 miles from Airdrie) shall upon getting due

DOI: 10.1057/9781137329844

intimation attend the funeral of a member or a member's wife in decent apparel or give a reasonable excuse to the satisfaction of the society under a penalty of 6/- for each neglect'.[36] The management was of a democratic nature: the executive committee included 12 members and was elected on a yearly basis.

However, the majority of mid-Victorian friendly societies were con-trolled by the Catholic Church whose aim was threefold: avoid Protestant contagion (by separating Catholics from their Protestants counterparts); preserve the faith; and promote respectability amongst parishioners. Thus confraternities were formed to maintain the Catholic faith in the 1860s: in Airdrie, there were four societies, namely The Living rosary; The Children of Mary; the Truce; and Our Lady of Perpetual Succour.[37] In Saint Lawrence's parish (Greenock), in 1868, the Living Rosary Sodality was composed of 6 circles of 15 members each and the Our Lady of Carmel Confraternity had 96 members.[38] Evening conferences were organized by parochial societies such as the Christian Doctrine Society (Airdrie), whose gatherings were praised by the Scottish local press: 'The varied entertainments, which showed...the advanced cultivation attained amongst the younger members of Saint Margaret's congregation'.[39]

Mixing and socializing between Catholics and Protestants was looked upon as a curse by clerical authorities – thus, Father McIntosh, curate of Saint Margaret since 1867, wrote to the Vicariate in the 1870s:

> Besides the heavy work which spreads over a wide area we are together deeply engaged in abolishing abuses prevailing in the Parish. The chief is company keeping with Protestants ending in marriages often at the kirks. We wage a furious war against these. They are the curse of the place.[40]

To prevent such gatherings, friendly societies for young people were a useful tool: the purpose of the Catholic Young Men's Association's (CYMA) was to educate and separate young Catholics from their Protestant workmates. In the 1860s, Greenock's CYMA, with 40 members, had opened a library where the latter could consult over 150 books as well as newspapers and journals.[41] The CYMA's administration was under clerical control, with its three golden rules being 'Monthly Communion; Chaplain's Veto; and No Party Politics'.[42]

Also, temperance was key to Victorian ethics and the Catholic Church tried to develop abstinence societies, although rules were often less strict than those of the Protestant organizations. For instance, the Airdrie

DOI: 10.1057/9781137329844

Catholic Association for the Suppression of Drunkeness in 1868 allowed for its members to drink two pints of malt liquor during working days and forbade all alcoholic beverages on religious duty days.

Irish Catholic societies, mainly church-based in the 1850s and 1860s, were somewhat transformed during the late Victorian era, with new identity-based associations being created. The parochial organisations, which dated back to the 1850s, continued to develop: for instance, in Airdrie, four confraternities were active (Living Rosary, Children of Mary, Holy Family, and the Sacred Heart Association) in the late 1890s.[43] Concerning temperance, the *Leagues of the Cross*, created in 1872 (their symbols and rewards followed that of the Salvation Army model), opened sections in Greenock (1,100 members in 1882) and in the Monklands.[44] Youth associations such as the CYMA organized winter conferences – in Airdrie a series of debates over historical issues took place in 1878, with the following themes under discussion: 'Was Mary, Queen of Scots, accessory to the murder of her husband Lord Darnley?'; 'Was Napoleon more ambitious than Oliver Cromwell?'; 'Was the execution of Charles I justifiable?'.[45]

The Irish National Foresters (INF) emerged in the late 1880s. Once accepted by the Catholic hierarchy, it developed in the West of Scotland: in 1890, there were 5,945 INF members in Scotland (who represented half of the total number of members in the United Kingdom).[46] Coatbridge was the first to inaugurate a 'Michael Davitt' section in 1886, with the following rules:

> This Branch shall have for its object the Raising of money by Contribution of Members, Entrance fees, and Donations for the following purposes: – 1st, paying a weekly allowance to Members when unable to follow their employment from sickness or accident; 2nd, for the decent burial of Members and their lawful married wives; 3rd, for supplying medical attendance and medicine to Members; 4th a Subsidiary Fund for the relief of Members in distressed circumstances.[47]

Thus, the Foresters' society appeared to be a typical friendly society – but what made it different from other previous Catholic organizations in Scotland was that membership was open only to the 'Irish by birth or by descent'.[48] Membership of the Coatbridge branch was around 200–300 Foresters in the late 1890s.[49] A few local prominent citizens presided the association. From 1886 to 1895, Charles O'Neill, Arthur Malone and John Benson were repeatedly elected Chief Rangers.[50] O'Neill, the Irish

DOI: 10.1057/9781137329844

nationalist leader, was even appointed in 1892 as the High Grand Chief Ranger at the annual Foresters' conference.[51] In adjacent Airdrie, the local Foresters' section, named after a deceased Scottish priest (James McIntosh Branch), opened in 1898.[52] The Greenock section was founded in 1887 (Owen Roe O'Neill) and had 250 members by 1895; the Foresters also opened a juvenile section in 1891.[53]

The INF's status was ambiguous: although it was originally meant as an Irish friendly society, it soon made contact with nationalist organizations. The exclusive Irish membership was fiercely watched over by leaders such O'Neill. He refused to accept non-Irish members as honorary members at the 1890 annual conference, by arguing that: 'it might place its business in the hands of Scotch and other people'.[54] Furthermore, the same Irishmen were to be found in the executives of the Foresters and of the Irish National Leagues, e.g. Hugh McGhee was treasurer of the Coatbridge League in 1888, 1895 and 1899 and also treasurer of the INF's local section in 1895. Even contemporaries seem to have been unable, at times, to distinguish between the two organizations: thus, the *Glasgow Observer* explained in July 1889 that the Irish League was 'political and patriotic' whereas the 'The Foresters is a patriotic society too, but it is for social, not political, ends that it has been organised', acknowledging at the same time that 'many Irishmen belong to both'.[55] A few years later, the Catholic press encouraged Irish membership: 'They were all ardent Home Rulers; therefore, if they wished the cause of Home Rule to prosper they should all enrol their names as members of the Irish National Foresters'.[56]

Regarding religious affiliation, the INF was not exclusively Catholic: thus, John Hutchinson, the Order's general secretary in Dublin stated that 'the objects (unity, nationality and benevolence)... uniting in one common bond of brotherhood all Irishmen, regardless of the country in which they toil or the altar at which they kneel'.[57] However, Protestants formed less than 1 per cent of the Foresters' total membership: in the three Scottish towns under examination, no Protestant enrolled. Although the society was not officially Catholic, the strong influence of the clergy on its organization would have debarred any Protestant. In fact, meetings were often held in Catholic school rooms or parish halls, and priests were honorary members who often chaired concerts and social events.

During the Edwardian era, the essence of Irish Catholic friendly societies did change with the rise of a different types of society such as the Ancient Order of Hibernians (AOH). In contrast with this exclusively Catholic society, the INF had to reassert their fundamental values and

DOI: 10.1057/9781137329844

principles, as the Coatbridge branch secretary declared in 1901: 'the Order is non-political and non-sectarian'.[58] The 1905 National Conference of the INF which took place in Motherwell, persisted in emphasizing that: 'Catholicity is not an essential principle of Irish Forestry, and though the members are almost exclusively Catholic, its ranks are open to all creeds'.[59] On the whole, as a friendly society promoting respectability and moral elevation, the INF certainly played a part in the integration of Irish migrants within Scottish society.[60] Patrick Agnew, one of the executives of the INF in Airdrie, stated in 1901:

> They were sometimes accused of copying their neighbours. It was true that they had to some extent copied the people they lived amongst and whom the fates had destined they should live amongst; but in Scotland they had built up an organization of a friendly society character which was second to no other in the country... He took it that today that would be accepted by their neighbours as a testimony that they had learned the lesson of self-reliance and thrift... The INF was the eldest Irish Friendly Society in the country.[61]

Whereas the Foresters were eager to put forward their tolerant attitude, the Ancient Order of Hibernians spread in the West of Scotland from the early 1900s onwards upon a different basis. Initially considered by the Church authorities as a secret society, it was subsequently acknowledged as a friendly society in the late 1890s, and the first reports on the activities of Hibernian branches were published in the Scottish Catholic press in 1903. In April 1904, the confraternity had pamphlets circulated after mass in various churches in order to expose the society's purpose – which was threefold: Catholicism ('preservation of God's holy religion in Ireland and protection of the Roman Catholic clergy'), mutual aid (as a registered friendly society) and nationalism ('fearless champion of Irish liberty at home and abroad').[62] Irish birth or origin was a requirement – thus, certain Protestants viewed the society as 'most powerful secret society organized in the interest of Irish nationalism and with an exclusively Roman Catholic membership'.[63] The AOH was successful in Coatbridge: in 1906, the Iron Burgh had three branches (No. 279; No. 273 and No. 276) and Airdrie (No. 320) and Greenock (No. 17) had one local division each.[64]

Celebrating Saint Patrick's Day

The annual celebration of Catholic Irishness, Saint Patrick's Day, was a complex phenomenon, where politics, religion and Irish identity

DOI: 10.1057/9781137329844

were celebrated in a single event.[65] On the evening of March the 17th, Irish gatherings celebrated the Pope, deplored 'oppressed' Ireland and rejoiced in the presence of prominent Protestant citizens. Looking at the Saint Patrick's Day festivities of the 1850s and the 1860s, two types of social meetings can be discerned. The 'official' celebration of Saint Patrick was fêted by local respectable Irish elites in the form of a supper under clerical supervision. In larger towns such as Greenock, there were also more modest gatherings organized within the parish by local Irish working men.[66] The second type of celebration related to the 'unofficial' Saint Patrick's Day whereby some Irishmen 'drown[ed] the shamrock in a drop of potheen' in pubs and on the streets, to the great annoyance of Scottish local authorities.

During the mid-Victorian era, for practical and financial reasons, Irish parishioners often formed a committee a few months before the 17th and invited the local clergy to preside the evening. Yet the Catholic authorities in Scotland were sometimes reluctant to participate in this manifestation of Irishness: thus in 1865, the hierarchy decided to postpone the celebration to the 22nd of March for Saint Patrick's Day happened to fall on Good Friday that year. A committee of parishioners in Airdrie decided to override this decision and were admonished by their parish priest, Duncan McNab: 'First, That the Church of God is wont to honour the saints by fasting, not by feasting, on the eves of their festival; secondly, That here the 16th of March is not the eve of Saint Patrick's Day this year ...'.[67] This refusal did not prevent 300 Irishmen from gathering on the 16th of March, headed by James McAuley, with '50 Protestants present'.[68]

After the 1860s, amongst the Irish diaspora, the festival became more respectable because of 'its move off the streets and the concentration on indoor events'.[69] This move 'indoors' was accompanied by a change in the nature of the event. Effectively, the annual Saint Patrick festival exemplified political leanings within the Irish communities. Was Saint Patrick's day 'hijacked' by the Irish nationalists from the 1870s onwards in an attempt to change the ceremony into a mass political rally or did the Church attempt to convey greater respectability to the event?[70] In the late Victorian era, two parallel ways of celebrating the Irish patron saint's day coexisted: on the one hand, there were the traditional parochial reunions under the auspices of the local clergy, and on the other hand, political reunions started to emerge as a result of the growth of Irish nationalism in Scotland.

DOI: 10.1057/9781137329844

However, there were notable differences amongst the three cities: in Greenock for instance, the Irish gatherings remained mainly under the control of priests.[71] One Highland clergyman, Alexander Taylor, Saint Mary's vicar (from 1880 onwards), was particularly instrumental in keeping at bay nationalist ideas. From the mid-1880s to 1900, Father Taylor chaired the yearly concert and avoided all political reference: for instance, he declared in 1886 that the aim of the reunion was not 'a struggle for the independence of Ireland in the meantime' but a fight for the independence of the congregation (because of its heavy debts).[72] Moreover, Father Taylor succeeded in inviting half of the Greenock Town Council members, and declared:

> I am quite sure that fifty years ago, or forty years, or thirty years or even twenty-five years ago, the like of this would not have happened; and had Provost Shankland been in the Provost chair then, and come to a gathering of this kind, I am very doubtful if some of his best friends would not have wished him to be consigned to a very warm climate indeed (laughter).[73]

In 1895 and 1896, the Greenock town councillors took part again in the Saint Patrick's Day celebrations – in 1897, police officers were also invited.[74]

Despite the preponderance of parochial celebrations, the local nationalists did attempt to organize a few political reunions on March 17th. The latter were a combination of political and religious stances, as Neil Brown, a prominent Catholic citizen stated in 1883:

> Some people objected to holding a political meeting upon the anniversary of Saint Patrick, but… nothing could be more religious and more holy than to take steps to free people from the service of bondage (Applause).[75]

By contrast, celebrating Saint Patrick's Day in the Monklands was a different matter altogether: as early as March 1875, 400 people paraded down the streets of Coatbridge and Airdrie and 1, 000 Irishmen gathered in the Airdrie Municipal Hall at a meeting chaired by James McAuley under the auspices of the local Home Rule Association. John Ferguson, the evening keynote speaker explained that this was Airdrie's 'first political demonstration' on Saint Patrick's Day.[76] In fact, until 1875 Saint Patrick celebrations in Airdrie consisted in concerts and dinners held in the parochial hall.[77] In Coatbridge the political tradition grew strong in the late nineteenth century. In March 1895, D. J. Sheahan, the organizer of the Irish National League in Britain addressed the Irish in Coatbridge

DOI: 10.1057/9781137329844

alongside M.P. William O'Brien.[78] As regards nationalist meetings, the Catholic clergy at times showed enthusiasm. For instance, in March 1883, Father Michael O'Keeffe (who described himself being 'hot temper[ed]') attended a gathering under the auspices of the local Irish league whereby he spoke of the 'Irish's race' and its 'just struggle for their legal rights'.[79] A few years later, in March 1886, both Father O'Keeffe and Father John Hughes (of Saint Augustine's, Coatbridge) agreed to resolutions supporting the Irish Parliamentary Party.[80]

When the monarchy ordered the wearing of the green to Irish soldiers and members of the government on March 17th, to celebrate the bravery of Irish regiments during the Second South African War (1899–1902), a certain amount of respectability was given to the organizers of Saint Patrick's Day celebrations. During the Edwardian era, local circumstances greatly determined the type of Saint Patrick celebration – in Greenock, Irish folklore and music took on more importance than nationalist claims whereas in Coatbridge, the Irish nationalists were still to the fore. At a Saint Patrick's gathering in 1908, Charles O'Neill declared before a Coatbridge audience:

> They were doing honour in the first instance to the patron saint of Ireland, Saint Patrick, and at the same time they were there to lend a helping hand to advance the cause of Irish national independence and to do all in their power to place Ireland in the same independent prosperous and flourishing condition in which Saint Patrick left it, following upon the introduction of Christianity by him into the land.[81]

During the prewar era, the impressive Saint Patrick meetings generally organized by the local branch of the United Irish League in Coatbridge were regularly reported in the press.[82] Yet this did not signify that parochial style Saint Patrick evenings had disappeared from the Monkland scene: for instance in March 1902, the Saint Vincent de Paul Society launched a concert in Coatbridge, and in March 1911, two balls were held in the parishes of Saint Margaret's and Saint Patrick's.[83]

The celebration of Saint Patrick's Day varied in time and in nature – depending on the degree of integration of the local Irish communities and on the attitude of the local priesthood, the celebration could turn into an urban fête to the sound of Irish music as it did in Greenock or a political nationalist manifesto as was the case in Coatbridge. On the whole, the celebration gained a certain degree of respectability over time and revealed different facets of Catholic Irishness.

DOI: 10.1057/9781137329844

Conclusion

The 1851–1914 period was a time when Catholic churches regained a position in the urban landscape unseen since the Reformation. Alongside
material aspects (finances, the building of churches and schools),
Catholic institutional life had to reinvent the way in which to fit into
nineteenth century Presbyterian Scotland. This chapter has shown that
the historical claim which ascribed to the Catholic Church the intention
to denationalize does not stand up to careful local scrutiny in Scotland.
First, a denationalization undertaking was not realistic in view of the
significant number of Irish priests, amongst whom there were staunch
nationalists. Second, the idea that the Church set out to denationalize
the Irish could be interpreted as giving too much importance to the late
nineteenth century concerns of Irish nationalists, who feared the influence of certain Scottish priests hostile to Irish nationalism. In fact, it has
been argued that the essential preoccupation of the Catholic Church
in the West of Scotland was to avoid a decrease in religious practice by
developing associational life and to increase its Irish flock's respectability
in the eyes of their Scottish hosts. Of course, the hierarchy condemned
any manifestation of radical nationalism but it turned a blind eye on Irish
clergymen participating in nationalist meetings. Moderate Irish Catholic
nationalism was thus seen as acceptable by the Church in Scotland.

Notes

1   T. Gallagher (1987) *Glasgow: The Uneasy Peace: Religious Tension in Modern
     Scotland* (Manchester: Manchester University Press), pp. 7–41.
2   The Western Vicariate being ruled by an Apostolic Vicar.
3   M.J. Hickman (1999) 'Alternative Historiographies of the Irish in Britain: A
     Critique of the Segregation/Assimilation Model' in R. Swift and S. Gilley (eds),
     The Irish in Britain: The Local Dimension (Dublin: Four Court Press), p. 247;
     M.J. Hickman (1992) 'Incorporating and Denationalizing the Irish in England:
     The Role of the Catholic Church' in P. O'Sullivan (ed.) *The Irish World Wide,
     vol. 5: Religion and Identity* (London: Leicester University Press), pp. 196–216.
4   On the issue of Catholic identities in Scotland, see S. Karly Kehoe (2011)
     'Unionism, Nationalism and the Scottish Catholic Periphery, 1850–1930',
     Britain and the World, 4, pp. 65–83.
5   GCA: History of the Missions of the Archdiocese, chap. XX, p. 76.
6   CD (1848), p. 71.

DOI: 10.1057/9781137329844

7   CD (1851), p. 89.

8   P. Drummond and P. Smith (eds) *Coatbridge: Three Centuries of Change*, Monklands Library Services Department, p. 34.

9   CD (1850).

10 CD (1835), p. 48. In order to accommodate the growing number of Catholics, another church (Saint Lawrence) was built in the Cartsdyke area in 1855 (1,300 parishioners) (see CD, 1861, pp. 96–7).

11 C. G. Brown (1997) *Religion and Society in Scotland since 1707* (Edinburgh: Edinburgh University Press), p. 192.

12 E. MacDonald (2004) 'The Gerards of Rochsoles Estate', *The Raddle*, 9, pp. 37–43.

13 NLA, U45/2/5/10.

14 *FP*, 12 November 1864.

15 CD (1867), p. 105.

16 H. M. Carey (2011) *God's Empire. Religion and Colonialism in the British World, c. 1801–1908* (Cambridge: Cambridge University Press), p. 27.

17 J. E. Handley (1943) *The Irish in Scotland* (Cork: Cork University Press), p. 204; B. Aspinwall (1996) 'Scots and Irish Ministering to Immigrants, 1830–1878', *Innes Review*, 47, p. 51.

18 V. A. McLlelland (1967) 'The Irish Clergy and Archbishop Manning's Apostolic Visitation of the Western District of Scotland, 1867. Part I: The Coming of the Irish', *The Catholic Historical Review*, LIII/1, p. 12.

19 V. A. McLlelland (1967) 'The Irish Clergy and Archbishop Manning's Apostolic Visitation', pp. 10–11.

20 SCA, OL/2/89/13.

21 See Appendix 2.

22 GAA, WD9, Murdoch's reply to the Address of the Clergy of the Western District, February 26, 1864.

23 SCA, SM15/4/5: Letter from Cardinal Barnabò (16 January 1868), quoted in Pastoral letter for the clergy and laity of Scotland, 28 January 1868.

24 Michael O'Keeffe (Coatbridge) was chairman of the '22' priests' committee which addressed a series of resolutions to Cardinal Barnabò, prefect of Fidei Propaganda in Rome (*FP*, 7 May 1864). One of the resolutions stated that: 'That while more than nineteenth twentieths of the faithful, and one half of the priests of the vicariate are by birth or parentage Irish, Scotch clergymen are nevertheless for the most part trustees of all our ecclesiastical properties, lands, churches, chapels'. SCA, DD2/28/9: Letter from Charles Muldoon to Michael Condon, 4 March 1868.

25 Airdrie Local Library: *Saint Margaret's Airdrie, 1836 to 1936* (Glasgow: John S. Burns), 1936, p. 9.

26 *AC*, 29 March 1862.

27 *FP*, 3 May 1862.

28 *FP*, 3 May 1862.

DOI: 10.1057/9781137329844

29   SCA, DD2/26/19: Letter from Charles Muldoon to Michael Condon, 10 September 1865.

30   *FP*, 3 December 1859.

31   SCA, OL/2/104/5–6: Letter by Michael O'Keeffe to Vicariate, 9 November 1862.

32   D. MacRaild (1999) *Irish Migrants in Modern Britain, 1750–1922* (London: Macmillan Press), p. 91.

33   GCA, TD/729/51.

34   GCA, TD/729/51.

35   GCA, TD/729/51.

36   GCA, TD/729/51.

37   CD (1869), p. 97.

38   *FP*, 14 April 1866.

39   *AC*, 5/1/1861.

40   GCA, GC/10/1/1: Letter from James McIntosh to Archdiocese, 2 March 1878.

41   SCA, WD/5/1.

42   T. Gallagher (1989). *Glasgow the Uneasy Peace*, pp. 54–5.

43   CD (1897), p. 184.

44   CD (1883), p. 105; CD (1891), p. 151.

45   *AC*, 28 September 1878; 26 October 1878; 30 November 1878.

46   *GO*, 9 August 1890.

47   NAS, FS 4/281: INF Michael Davitt, Rules of the Branch *Michael Davitt*, No. 86 (opened 6 December 1886), 1913.

48   *GO*, 27 July 1889.

49   *GO*, 25 May 1895.

50   *GO*, 25 May 1895.

51   *AC*, 15 August 1892.

52   *GE*, 10 December 1898.

53   *GO*, 7 December 1895; *GO*, 18 May 1895.

54   *GO*, 9 August 1890.

55   *GO*, 27 July 1889.

56   *GO*, 21 April 1894.

57   *GO*, 2 November 1889.

58   *GE*, 2 February 1901.

59   *GE*, 12 August 1905.

60   *AC*, 4 October 1902.

61   *CE*, 19 June 1901.

62   *GE*, 2 April 1904.

63   *AC*, 13 July 1912: Report from the Belfast Presbytery (4 July 1912).

64   *GE*, 30 June 1906.

65   D. MacRaild (2011) *The Irish Diaspora in Britain, 1750–1939* (Basingstoke: Palgrave Macmillan), pp. 85–6.

DOI: 10.1057/9781137329844

66 See letter by Michael Condon written in March 1865 to Vicariate: 'Numbers of my people, excluded from the supper by the high-priced tickets or the want of accommodation' (SCA, DD/2/26/3).

67 *FP*, 11 March 1865 : Letter from Duncan McNab to James Montgomery.

68 *AC*, 18 April 1865.

69 Mike Cronin, Daryl Adair (2002) *The Wearing of the Green. A History of St. Patrick's Day* (London: Routledge), p. 60.

70 D. MacRaild (2010) *The Irish Diaspora*, p. 65.

71 In the neighbouring town of Paisley, some priests refused to participate in the gatherings organized by the Irish National League. In 1896, Father Mullin explained during a meeting of the local St Mirrin's League of the Cross that he preferred to take part in parochial celebrations under clerical supervision (*GO*, 16 May 1896).

72 *GT*, 18 March 1886.

73 *GT*, 17 March 1894.

74 *GO*, 23 March 1895; *GT*, 17 March 1896; *GT*, 18 March 1897.

75 *GA*, 17 March 1883.

76 *AC*, 20 March 1875.

77 *AC*, 22 March 1873; 21 March 1874; 20 March 1875.

78 *GO*, 23 March 1895; *CE*, 20 March 1895.

79 GAA, GC/9/13/6: Letter from Michael O'Keeffe to Archbishop Eyre, 14 November 1877; *AC*, 24 March 1883.

80 *AC*, 20 March 1886.

81 *CL*, 21 March 1908.

82 *CE*, 21 March 1906.

83 *CE*, 19 March 1902; *AC*, 25 March 1911.

DOI: 10.1057/9781137329844

4
Educating the Irish Catholics

Abstract: *The historian John McCaffrey wrote that 'the educational system retained many of its traditional features and continued to mark out Scottish life in significant ways'. Thus it is central to study Irish Catholic activity within this key feature of Scottish national life. This chapter explores the founding of Catholic schools as well as Irish Catholic participation on School Boards – their local electoral strategies, Scotch-Irish disputes on the School Boards and the effectiveness of the maintenance of a separate Catholic schooling system. Paradoxically, although Irish Catholic ratepayers did not allow for the transfer of their schools to the state system before 1918, they nevertheless became deeply involved in the management of Scottish public education for financial reasons.*

Vaughan, Geraldine. *The 'Local' Irish in the West of Scotland, 1851–1921.* Basingstoke: Palgrave Macmillan, 2013. DOI: 10.1057/9781137329844.

DOI: 10.1057/9781137329844

No matter how carefully a Catholic child may be watched over by its parents, there will always be danger to its faith and morals from the class books used in Protestant schools, from the grooves of thought of its schoolmates, and more particularly from the tone and authority of the teacher.[1]

This extract from a letter sent to the *Free Press* in 1862 summarized how Catholics felt towards schooling. It was the role of the Church to save its parishioners from Protestant influence and provide early religious instruction.

Separating the Irish Catholics from Scottish society?

From the 1850s, the Catholic Church could rely on some state aid to develop its schools, providing that the latter were regularly inspected. Before compulsory schooling (1872), the Vicariate developed strategies to ensure that Irish children attended primary classes for at least a few years. The first reports on Airdrie's Catholic schools indicated that in 1856, 120 pupils attended the boys' school under the direction of the schoolmaster James McAuley and four monitors.[2] The pupils were divided into seven classes in half circles, and the inspector noted that 'the general condition of this school is creditable to the masters, and decidedly above the average of schools inspected for the first time'.[3] In Airdrie's girls' school, 80 pupils were in attendance, under the supervision of one mistress and three monitors: the school was divided into four classes, except for religious instruction and geography.

In October 1869, Father Condon in Greenock enumerated 476 children of school age (between 5 and 13) in Cartsdyke, with only half of them (270) attending the local Catholic school.[4] Moreover, the competition with Protestant schools was tough: in 1863, over 200 Catholic pupils attended the Greenock Protestant Ragged school.[5] In 1870 Coatbridge, four pence a fortnight were deducted from every miner's salary to pay for the upkeep of the local Protestant parochial school – in protest, a Catholic correspondent complained in the local press that a sixth of the 300 miners were Catholics and that they had to pay double fees (since their children attended the Catholic school).[6] However, attempting to assess accurately

DOI: 10.1057/9781137329844

the numbers of Catholic children going to Protestant schools is uneasy: the Church kept quiet about those considered 'relapsed' even though, from time to time, denunciations were made in the Catholic press.[7]

What was specific about Catholic primary schools?[8] A survey of the syllabuses of different schools in the Monklands shows that in Catholic schools no Latin or Greek was taught. Instead more practical subjects such as geography, algebra, navigation, and surveying were studied.[9] James McAuley, the local Irish politician, started out as a teacher in Airdrie in the early 1830s. One pupil remembered how he 'made use of the Protestant translation of the Bible to instruct his pupils so that they would not be unfamiliar with the version used by their fellow townsfolk'; he also 'provided classes in navigation and surveying.'[10]

Of course, religious instruction was fundamental to clergymen and teachers. The headmaster of Saint Lawrence primary Catholic school (Greenock) wrote in his logbook in January 1866 that 'the teacher confines himself to Religious Instruction which he believes is the most important, though he does not omit to mix during the week his lessons with religion'.[11] Catholic catechism stressed the learning of prayers and religious commandments.[12] Yet some Irish parents did not seem to value religious education, as reported in 1865 by a Greenock school director: 'It is to be regretted that parents do not take more interest in sending out their children to catechism... [They] are against teaching anything but reading and spelling until they are proficient in both.'[13]

As regards Catholic schooling, Mary Hickman has argued that the Church's policy was to 'denationalize' the Irish Catholic children:

> The strategies of incorporation which the Church developed, in particular Catholic education, aimed to regulate the expression and development of Irish identity. The particular focus was changing the identity of Irish pupils in Catholic schools... The identity of Irish working-class children as Catholics was implanted and constantly reinforced in the schools by the priority placed on religious instruction.[14]

Indeed, the Church was eager to maintain the children's Catholic identity – but in a Presbyterian land like Scotland, this did not help efforts at assimilation. Furthermore, Ireland was not ignored in the school's curriculum: for instance, one can infer from Saint Lawrence's logbook that essays on the subject of Ireland were regularly handed in.[15] Schools were also created to teach reading and writing to working-class children who attended quite irregularly and whose parents preferred

DOI: 10.1057/9781137329844

they miss religious instruction classes rather than arithmetic lessons. Thus Hickman's statement probably fits better the English case than the Scottish one, as strengthening these children's Catholic identity did not seem a wise move towards incorporation in a Presbyterian land.

Irish Catholics and School Boards, 1872–1900

With the passing of the Education (Scotland) Act in 1872, the former parish and burgh schools were transferred to a more coherent and centralized system of local government. Under this new system, Scottish schools were administered by locally elected School Boards under the supervision of the Scotch Education Department. As opposed to England, where a large voluntary sector survived the 1870 Education Act, in Scotland the vast majority of schools decided to join the state system in order to receive rate aid. Most of those who remained outside were Episcopalian and Roman Catholic. Although they did not benefit from the new public schooling system, Catholics, as ratepayers, wished to control the spending of their local taxes. Accordingly they became members of School Boards, thus offering a paradoxical example of voluntary participation in local government structures.[16]

The Catholic Church refused to transfer its schools into the public system because it was considered as 'denominational'. In contrast with English public schools, in Scottish burgh schools, religious education was systematically taught. In the overwhelming majority of schools, the Shorter Catechism (Presbyterian) was adopted – although parents who objected could withdraw their children during the religious education hours (which where scheduled to take place before or after school hours). Catholics considered that the whole School Board system was Presbyterian.[17] A Catholic journalist in 1888 summarized the paradoxical attitude of the Irish: 'we are obliged by law to build and maintain Board schools; and by conscience we are obliged to build schools in which our children may become acquainted with the tenets of the true faith'.[18]

Irish Catholic involvement in School Boards was occasionally viewed as an 'intrusion' by their Scottish counterparts. Firstly, Protestant prejudices concerning the ignorance of Catholics were still vivid. In the local press, a letter entitled 'Paddy's opinion of schoolmasters and school boards' portrayed Paddy arguing against the 'skool boords' power. 'The master says the skool boards and the big man in London will make us

DOI: 10.1057/9781137329844

[send them to school]', wrote Paddy, whereas this expenditure would be better spent on 'a drop of the crathur'.[19] Secondly, the cumulative vote favoured 'minorities' and Scottish citizens were agreed that the number of Catholic representatives should be kept fairly small.[20] For instance, in 1885, the *Greenock Telegraph* declared, 'It is not tolerable that the School Board of Greenock, a town with 80% of Protestants, should be invaded by Roman Catholics'.[21] Although several bills and petitions aimed at abolishing the cumulative vote in the late nineteenth century, the school board voting system remained the same. This irritated certain Scotsmen, as shown in the following 1900 invective:

> Minorities should scramble on to School Boards by ordinary means same as they do on other boards... Under a system of single voting I would have supported one or two of them [Roman Catholics], but under such a system it is certain we should not have had so many as four.[22]

However, Scots were often impressed by Catholic electoral organization: the cumulative vote, added to a comprehensive electoral organization, resulted in a consistent representation of the Catholic body on School Boards.[23] The voting franchise (£4 per annum) ensured a large number of the Irish flock, consisting mainly of labourers, could go to the poll. On polling day, Catholics revealed their well-thought-out organization – in 1891, the committee in charge of the Catholic vote in Coatbridge ensured that one of its members, to avoid the loss of a voter, 'took his place at one of the iron furnaces... while the voter went off to the polling station, which was quite far away'.[24] The energy spent in canvassing was acknowledged by Protestant citizens, as is evidenced in a 1900 newspaper commenting on the high scores of the Catholic candidates in the Old Monkland School Board election: 'the spoils of the election are to those who canvass hardest'.[25] Moreover, if the Catholics made sure to return at least two or three representatives on the Greenock and Monklands School Boards, they also fought for Catholic members being appointed in place of retiring or deceased Catholic members. In 1881, when James McAuley, the Catholic member of the Old Monkland and Airdrie School Boards died, another Catholic was appointed in his place. The Old Monkland School Board agreed to the decision taken by Catholic ratepayers that Father O'Reilly should be co-opted in place of McAuley.[26] This attitude appears to have remained a general practise at the Greenock and Monkland boards during the late Victorian period.

DOI: 10.1057/9781137329844

Although the local Liberal press had campaigned against clerical candidates in the months preceding the first School Board elections in 1873, ministers and priests soon became involved in the newly elected bodies. As the *Glasgow Observer* remarked in 1889, 'We can return our representatives to the Boards where they will be useful in many ways. In most cases the Catholic representative is the Reverend manager of the schools in the district.'[27] Thus, the Catholic Church played an active role through its clergymen, by lending parochial schools and halls to hold meetings, approving candidates and so on. For instance, in 1891, Michael O'Keeffe, senior priest of St Patrick's, gave the use of his schoolroom to the Catholic electoral committee and attended its meetings every night. In May 1906, a meeting of Saint Augustine's congregation was convened by the clergy one Sunday after mass in Saint Augustine school and presided by Frs. Müller and O'Herlihy.[28] Some priests went as far as to contradict the local Catholic political agenda – in April 1897, during the Old Monkland School Board electoral campaign, John Hughes, senior priest of Saint Augustine's, Coatbridge, opposed Arthur Malone, an Irish Catholic candidate, on the grounds that the latter was a spirit merchant. Father Hughes gave his full support to John Donaldson, a miner's agent.[29] Malone lost the election, and Donaldson was elected along with two other Catholics.

Catholic mobilization did not prevent divisions and tensions within the Catholic electoral body. In Greenock, Catholics in 1879 fought over the nomination of Robert Cook, a pawnbroker. Some argued that he was 'put forward by the extreme nationalist party' and was therefore not 'the nominee of the Catholic body'.[30] The tension was obvious again in 1880 when the local paper reported that 'there [has been] a rupture in the Catholic body ever since the School Board *fracas*'.[31] In Coatbridge, during the 1894 School Board elections, tensions emerged within the clerical body. Father John McCay, of Saint Patrick's, wrote to Provost Maguire: 'Father Hughes, unless prevented by you, is probably going to throw out the three candidates unanimously elected by the five priests concerned in the election.'[32] McCay asked for the Archdiocese's intervention to avoid 'a scandal – division among Catholics and the humiliation of the Catholic candidates'.[33]

Once Catholic candidates had secured a seat on the various school boards, disputes could arise with their Scottish colleagues. The first sensitive debate that cropped up with the forming of School Boards was that of the opening prayer. This was an issue in many Western School Boards

DOI: 10.1057/9781137329844

in Scotland: at the Old Monkland School Board, unusually, the motion in favour of a prayer was defeated at is first meeting, by James McAuley, along with four other (Protestant) members.[34] The situation was different in Airdrie: in January 1876, at a New Monkland School Board meeting, it was resolved to open the meetings with a prayer, and as a member, J. Wilson, put it: '[u]s Scotch people like to commence proceedings of this kind with a prayer'.[35] In Greenock, the issue was regularly debated by Catholic and Protestant members: in 1886, Father Michael Condon proposed an amendment to the public prayer rule, arguing on a theological basis that Catholics could not pray in communion with Protestants.[36] Condon's amendment was defeated, but three years later Father O'Reilly, who had topped the poll in the election, described this position as reactionary:

> For the support of the Board schools all denominations are taxed... and when elected all denominations are equal. But soon as we come here the equality is removed; Christian charity is flung to the wind... It reminds me of the select cast of the Brahmins in India who consider their prayers to be so pleasing and persuasive with God, that no one else need try to pray... Such a scandal is worthy of the dark ages, and altogether unbecoming in this nineteenth century.[37]

After years of battling, a compromise was reached in 1891: from then on, the Board's chairman simply said a few words of prayer before the start of a public meeting.[38]

School Boards were divided into various committees, dealing with attendance, finances, management, building and religious instruction. As elected members, Catholics were chosen to attend or chair different committees except, of course, that of the (Protestant) religious instruction committee. Hugh O'Hear, a Catholic member of the Old Monkland School Board, jokingly remarked in April 1900, when the 'religions teaching committee' was formed, amongst whose members there were one Protestant minister and one Orangeman: 'That's a committee of good Protestants (laughter)'.[39] As a rule, Catholic clergymen were appointed to the schools' committees of management because of their experience as school directors. For instance, in April 1882, Father Thomas O'Reilly was appointed to the committee of Faskine school (Airdrie). Another member, Mr Allan, commented that he 'also thought that Mr O'Reilly would make an efficient member of the school committee, as the Catholic schools were conducted on a much cheaper scale'.[40] Since the Education Act imposed school attendance on all children aged between 5 and 13, School Boards

DOI: 10.1057/9781137329844

had the power to prosecute defaulting parents, whether the children were going to public or voluntary schools. Thus Catholic members were also often appointed members of the Attendance Committee.

As pointed out earlier, the involvement of (Irish) Catholics was paradoxical: they engaged in a structure which had virtually no power over Catholic schools, yet their initial aim was solely to control public expenditure. Indeed, the financial incentive was a trigger to their participation: as ratepayers, the Catholics wanted public money to be cautiously spent. This, in effect, was a major electoral argument: as the Catholic *Glasgow Observer* put it in 1888, there was nobody 'more careful and economising than the Catholic members'.[41] Accordingly, Catholic members tried to save money in various ways: for example, at the Greenock School Board, in 1892, John Brown, a Catholic member, convinced the Board to give up the distribution of religious book prizes (paid for by the Board) arguing that it was unfair on a large section of ratepayers. Father Murphy further added that 'Some people did state Scriptural reasons for refusing money from the public rates for religious instruction, but he had no such objection – (laughter) – he would be only too glad to take a share of the public rates for that purpose at any time (renewed laughter).'[42] During the late nineteenth century, Scottish members of School Boards were willing to acknowledge the work accomplished by Catholic members. For example, in September 1881, the chairman of the Old Monkland School Board, John Alexander, lauded the late James McAuley's 'most regular attendance and intelligent part in all the business and arrangements necessary for carrying on the work of the Board'.[43] Of course, the laudatory dimension of obituaries of this kind should be treated with caution. Nevertheless, careful attention paid to the School Board reports in the local press and minute books reveal that Catholics were quite regular in their attendance at the general and committee meetings and willing to collaborate, give advice or oppose other members.

Disputes on School Boards during the Edwardian era

In preparation for the 1906 School Board elections, *The Glasgow Examiner* published the following reminder to its readers:

> Because the School Board has power to prosecute defaulting parents (Catholics as well as non-Catholics)… Because the School Board has power to provide for the education of poor, blind etc. and truant of all

DOI: 10.1057/9781137329844

denomination… Because Catholic representation on School Boards was never more important than at the present time, when under the guise of so-called 'Secular Education' an attempt is made to banish from all public schools the teaching of religion and christian morals.[44]

Thus, during the prewar years, the Irish Catholics were assigned a new task of putting forward 'Christian' values within the boards. From a Scottish point of view, School Boards were a key institution, not only because they supervised Scottish education but also because they were perceived as somewhat autonomous bodies: 'with strong minds at the School Board there is always hope of making head against purely London control'.[45]

During the Edwardian era, Irish Catholics usually managed to be represented on School Boards by at least two members. The Old Monkland School Board was where Catholics scored the highest: by 1918, the latter even claimed that 'the Catholic body has always returned four members to the Old Monkland School Board'.[46] In educational affairs, it seemed that the interests of the Catholic Church came first. The editor of *The Glasgow Observer*, D. J. Mitchel Quin, wrote in 1913 that 'at the School Board Election the Irish vote goes for the Catholic members, naturally and properly, and Labour is left to its own resources'.[47] However, Labour did manage to put forward some candidates, for example, Paul McKenna, a miners' agent of Irish descent, ran for election as a Labour candidate to the Airdrie School Board in April 1914 (one of his electoral slogans was: 'Workers vote for McKenna').[48] He was elected and even topped the poll with 3047 votes.[49] Of course, this was possible thanks to the Catholic vote, for he was supported by St Margaret's parishioners, the parish to which he himself belonged. Electoral support for the Catholics even came from the Scottish Protestants, a situation ill-appreciated by the Church of Scotland pastor, Jacob Primmer, well-known for his anti-Catholic views.[50] Before a Coatbridge audience in July 1901, he thundered: 'it is a disgrace… that in Coatbridge there should be four Papists looking after the education of their Protestant children… while Protestants vote for them!'.[51]

In April 1906, an argument over the setting of the Christmas holidays led to a dispute on religious grounds in the Old Monkland School Board. Father Hackett suggested there should be a 15-day vacation running from December 21 to January 7, but the Board's chairman was opposed to the motion, saying 'we d[o] not keep Christmas in Scotland'.[52] Father Hackett reacted violently: 'this was supposed to be a Christian country', he said,

DOI: 10.1057/9781137329844

'The King's birthday and Primrose Day were observed, and the birthday of our Lord could not be observed. They were going out to teach children. No wonder we had heathens.'[53] The Baptist member Samuel Lindsay, then set out to teach Catholic members something about Scottishness: 'Might I remind the Board that Protestant Scotland – the land that is famed all over the world for its pure religion – puts no value on 'days, and months and times and years', as these apply themselves too often to superstitious customs.'[54]

One particularly heated point of contention discussed on the various boards was the question of free books: the controversy lasted from 1908 to 1910. This issue first came under examination when the new Education Act for Scotland (1908) made provision for the free supply of books, food and clothing to necessitous children. This act conferred power on the School Boards to extend measures of help to voluntary schools, but these powers were permissive, not mandatory.[55] Catholic members of the Old Monkland School Board argued in favour of Voluntary school children getting free books, but Protestant members objected: 'where public money was being spent there should be some public control' – no free books should be distributed to schools that had chosen to remain independent.[56] Catholics argued that, by keeping their schools 'off the rates', they were saving the ratepayers '£4000 per annum'.[57] The irony was that when Catholics finally won the battle of free books for needy children attending Catholic schools in 1910, they realized that the School Board books could not be used in Catholic schools.[58]

In the opinion of some ultra-Protestant members, Catholics were given too many crucial positions. In 1911, the Baptist councillor Samuel Lindsay, of the Old Monkland School Board, complained that two Catholics had been given key convenerships, respectively the 'Staffing and Attendance Committee' and the 'Technical and Evening Continuation Schools Committee'.[59] His argument was that these two gentlemen 'in the nature of their relationship to the public schools, had the smallest interest in the success of Protestant teachers and pupils'.[60]

Conclusion

On the eve of the outbreak of the First World War, the Catholic education issue had become one of the main hobby-horses of the Catholic

DOI: 10.1057/9781137329844

community. In June 1914, Father Hackett predicted to the Old Monkland Board:

> It was only a question of time when they would have their rights in spite of everything... They had the same inspectors, the same code, the same books, and the same time-table, but because they taught their children a different catechism they were deprived a share of the grant... This is a free country, and it is the boast of Protestant countries that there is freedom within their borders, but where is the freedom there?[61]

Notes

1   *FP*, 29 November 1862.
2   CD (1856), p. 95: Inspector's report: St Margaret's schools, examined 20th June, 1854.
3   CD (1856), p. 95
4   CD (1873), p. 17 ; CD (1871), p. 108.
5   *FP*, 21 November 1863.
6   *AC*, 24 September 1862.
7   *FP*, 22 November 1862.
8   Secondary education was not a priority for the nineteenth century Catholic Church in Scotland. There were exceptions such as Saint Mary's Academy, which was inaugurated in Greenock in 1864. History, geometry, Latin, Greek and French were part of the syllabus.
9   GCA, TD/729/7: *Some Aspects of Schools and Schooling in the Monklands before 1873*.
10   Airdrie Library : *Saint Margaret's Airdrie, 1836 to 1936*.
11   GCA, CO/2/5/6/86/1: *St Lawrence's R. C. school logbook*, 27 January 1866.
12   GCA, CO/2/5/6/86/1: *St Lawrence's R. C. school logbook*, 26 October 1869.
13   GCA, CO/2/5/6/86/1: *St Lawrence's R. C. school logbook*, 9 June 1865 and 17 June 1865.
14   M. Hickman (1999) 'Alternative Historiographies of the Irish in Britain: A Critique of the Segregation/Assimilation Model' in R. Swift and S. Gilley (eds), *The Irish in Britain : The Local Dimension* (Dublin: Four Court Press), pp. 241–42.
15   GCA, CO/2/5/6/86/1: *St Lawrence's R. C. school logbook*, 31 May 1865.
16   G. Vaughan (2012) '"Papists looking after the Education of our Protestant Children !" Catholics and Protestants on Western Scottish School Boards, 1872–1918', *The Innes Review*, 63, pp. 30–47.
17   *GE*, 28 September 1895.
18   *GO*, 3 April 1888.

DOI: 10.1057/9781137329844

19 *AC*, 6 March 1875.
20 The cumulative vote allowed one voter to cast several votes (as many votes as there were candidates) on one or several candidates.
21 *GT*, 25 March 1885.
22 *AC*, 14 April 1900.
23 The Old Monkland School Board dealt with Coatbridge's schools; the New Monkland and Airdrie School Boards dealt with schools in Airdrie and its surroundings.
24 *GO*, 18 April 1891.
25 *AC*, 7 April 1900. The four Roman Catholic candidates arrived in the 3rd, 5th, 7th and 9th position (respectively, Father Hughes with 4672 votes; Hugh O'Hear with 4334 votes; Charles O'Neill with 4245 votes and Father Kirke with 4080 votes).
26 GCA, CO1/5/1/8/2: *Minute Book of Old Monkland School Board, 1880–1884*, p. 108.
27 *GO*, 3 March 1889.
28 *CE*, 29 May 1906
29 GAA, GC/29/95: Letter from Charles O'Neill to Archbishop, 15 December 1897.
30 *GA*, 22 March 1879.
31 *GA*, 26 October 1880.
32 GAA, GC/26/14/4: Letter from John McCay to Provost Maguire, March 1894.
33 GAA, GC/26/14/4: Letter from John McCay to Provost Maguire, March 1894.
34 See for instance, the Renton school board case (Alexandria), where a Catholic clergyman attempted to move that meetings should not start with prayers, as they were dealing with secular issues. His motion was defeated, and meetings started with a ten minute opening prayer (*GO*, 19 May 1888). See also *AC*, 26 April 1873.
35 *AC*, 29 January 1876.
36 *GT*, 17 April 1885; *GT*, 8 May 1885.
37 *GT*, 8 June 1888.
38 *GT*, 20 April 1894.
39 *CE*, 18 April 1900.
40 *AC*, 22 April 1882.
41 *GO*, 7 April 1888.
42 *GT*, 5 February 1892.
43 GCA, CO1/5/1/8/2: *Minute Book of Old Monkland School Board, 1880–1884*, p. 98.
44 *GE*, 24 March 1906.
45 *GT*, 2 April 1914.

DOI: 10.1057/9781137329844

46   *CE*, 20 February 1918.
47   GAA, GC45/68: Letter from D. J. Mitchel Quin to George Barns, MP, 15 April 1913.
48   *AC*, 11 April 1914.
49   *CL*, 11 April 1914.
50   Jacob Primmer (1842–1914) preached around Scotland every summer from 1890 to 1903. See T. Gallagher (1987) *Glasgow: The Uneasy Peace: Religious Tension in Modern Scotland* (Manchester: Manchester University Press), pp. 35–6.
51   *CE*, 10 July 1901.
52   *CE*, 28 November 1909.
53   *CE*, 28 November 1909.
54   *CE*, 26 December 1906.
55   J. Handley (1947) *The Irish in Modern Scotland* (Cork : Cork University Press), p. 236.
56   *CL*, 2 May 1908.
57   *CL*, 19 February 1910.
58   *CL*, 3 December 1910.
59   *CL*, 8 April 1911.
60   *CL*, 8 April 1911.
61   *CL*, 20 June 1914.

DOI: 10.1057/9781137329844

5
Local Politics

Abstract: *Chapter 5 uncovers a long neglected aspect of the historiography of the Irish in Scotland, namely their involvement in local politics. It argues that participation in municipal politics was decisive in terms of integration for Irish migrants as well as in determining part of the local political history of Scotland. Browsing through a large selection of archival material, this chapter explains how Irish migrants became involved in parochial and municipal councils. It also explores divisions within the Irish Catholic community on local issues, thus reassessing and revisiting W.M. Walker's argument that Catholics were priest-ridden.*

Vaughan, Geraldine. *The 'Local' Irish in the West of Scotland, 1851–1921.* Basingstoke: Palgrave Macmillan, 2013. DOI: 10.1057/9781137329844.

Local government was a major feature of Scottishness during the Victorian and Edwardian eras.[1] Since key national decisions were taken down in London, the power devolved to local institutions represented a form of self-administration. As Thomas Devine has demonstrated, along with other Scottish historians including Richard Finlay and Lindsay Paterson, the stateless nation had control at a local level, 'where it mattered most to people in the Victorian period, that is at the level of the city, the burgh and the locality'.[2]

The Catholic Irish and parish councils

The first institutions conquered by the Irish were parochial boards (which became parish councils in 1894). These boards were in charge of the administration of the 1845 New Poor Law – they assessed rates, decided on the amount of relief distributed and supervised the internal arrangements of the poorhouses.[3] The provision of outdoor and indoor relief was granted to disabled poor who could justify five years' residence within the parish. Regarding parochial elections, few Irishmen could run in the 1850s as representatives as they had to be both ratepayers and nominated by an assembly of ratepayers. In Greenock, the continuity of early Catholic representation on the parochial board was ensured by one man, Patrick O'Neill, who was elected councillor from 1850 to 1868.[4] After 1868 there were a maximum of two Irish representatives on the Board – as Allison, a Scots councillor, remarked: 'it was obvious that the Irish population was a fourth and they only had two representatives'.[5] In the Monklands, Irish Catholic representation was slightly higher: for instance, in 1863, there were three Catholic members (Hugh O'Hear, Henry McLachlan and Mark Kennedy) on the Old Monkland Parochial Board.[6]

The aim of Irish Catholic representatives was to defend their poor and preserve Catholic children from Protestant influence. The issues they dealt with regarded the churching of Roman Catholic poorhouse inmates, the boarding out of Catholic children into Protestant families, the paying of school rates for pauper Catholic children, and the internment of Catholic paupers. On account of the migratory nature of Irish labour, there were numerous Irish applying for relief who could not fill the settlement clause, as Robert Wright, a parochial councillor of Greenock observed in 1852:

DOI: 10.1057/9781137329844

It was well known that the applications were numerous from the Irish poor who had been but a short time here, and it was a complaint from members of the Relief Committee that they could not put the test of the Poor house to these parties as they wished, seeing Mr O'Neill was sitting there, and was ready to accuse them of partiality if they did not also test the poor applicants who were natives of the town.[7]

Scottish councillors often found fault with the great number of Irish applicants. For instance, the Greenock Inspector of Poor in 1869 proposed the 'extension of the period of residence settlement from five to seven years' before a parliamentary commission.[8] Indeed, in the early 1860s, the Irish represented over 40 per cent of the poorhouse inmates in Airdrie and Greenock. In the 1880s, controversies on the greater proportion of Irish poor in need of relief still arose in the councils – for instance, in 1882, the 'Ann O'Hara case' in Greenock showed that national and religious tensions still ran high. Ann O'Hara was an 'an Irishwoman without any settlement in Greenock or other parish in Scotland' who was to be removed to Ireland, but who escaped from the police conducting her to the boat on several occasions.[9] Her case led the Inspector of Poor to complain to the Board of 'how far [they] as a community are burdened by Irish paupers'.[10] He further remarked on how short the five-year residence clause seemed, as 'there were many Irish in the parish who notwithstanding their nationality had acquired a settlement'.[11]

Rejected pauper applicants faced deportation. In 1860, a Belfast manufacturer wrote in the *Free Press* the story of Patrick Malone, a 32 year-old Irish labourer, who hailed from County Monaghan. Malone had started out working in the Shotts Ironwork from 1852 to 1856; he then worked in Glasgow for a year and a half before settling in Calderbank (Old Monkland). Once he was out of work, he was admitted to the poorhouse in Glasgow, and then removed to Belfast where one manufacturer helped him pay his passage back to Scotland.[12] Patrick Malone's case was by no means uncommon, as deported Irish often took the ferry back to Scotland.[13] Parochial boards frequently protested against the costs of deportation – in 1868, the Greenock board agreed to: 'to bring up a report before an early meeting what sum the English, Scotch and Irish ratepayers respectively contribute to the Greenock Parochial Board... and what it cost this Board in passage money and expenses to send back applicants to Ireland'.[14] The efficiency of deportation to Ireland was still questioned in the late nineteenth century. White, a Scottish representative at the Old Monkland Parish Council, stated in 1896 that 'after spending the best of

DOI: 10.1057/9781137329844

their days in this country, being sent back in their old age to their native land, which after such a length of time was practically a wilderness to them to live in'.[15]

Protecting Catholic pauper children against Protestant influence was another concern. With orphans, religious education was at stake as there was a debate on whether orphans should be educated in the religion of their deceased parents or if it was it for the public authorities to decide. In Greenock a controversy arose in 1850 over Father James Danaher's complaint to the Board of Supervision that he was denied the right to teach catechism to Poorhouse Catholic children.[16] The Greenock Board refused to grant this permission to the priest, on account of a previous resolution.[17] In order to cancel this motion, the Irish Catholic members of the board decided to argue their case to the central government – and the Board of Supervision invalidated the decision of the Greenock board.[18] Yet there were further discussions on the religious denominations of orphans – and Greenock's Inspector of Poor argued that the children kept in the poorhouse were too young to have yet formed 'religious opinions for themselves'.[19] Again, the Board of Supervision decided to support the Catholic argument, namely to register children according to their parents' religious beliefs because 'children should be entered as of religious persuasion to which their parents were known to belong'.[20] Conversely, the local Scottish press supported local authorities versus the central government. For instance, the *Glasgow Sentinel* stated in 1850 that 'The Greenock Board are pretty general in the opinion that, in dictating this course, the higher board are travelling beyond their power'.[21]

Yet the Greenock Parochial Board found other tactics to enable 'Catholic' orphans to be raised as Protestants 'by boarding out in the country the children registered as Roman Catholics'.[22] In the Monklands, the same kind of debate took place, but although the Parochial Boards allowed for the children's religion to be registered on their entry at the Poorhouse, they 'denied, that, having done so, there was any obligation that children registered as Catholics should be allowed to be educated as such'.[23] In fact, according to the New Monkland Board in 1853, deserted children of Catholic parents were to be 'entered, taught, and treated as Protestants'.[24] However, after the request made by a Scottish Catholic member of the Board, Sir Archibald Gerard of Rochsoles, the New Monkland Parochial Board had to withdraw this motion. The disputes that had arisen over the handling of Catholic orphans in the 1850s and 1860s were dissipated from the late 1870s onwards. There were still

DOI: 10.1057/9781137329844

occasional debates at the Greenock Parochial Board, for instance in 1882, when the two Catholic members demanded that Catholic orphans be sent to Smyllum, the Catholic orphanage, on the grounds that it would save the parish money as opposed to boarding out the children in Scottish families.[25] Yet the Scottish members were in favour of boarding out the children in the countryside, for as one of them, Kerr, remarked: 'it was so difficult to get parents of the Roman Catholic religion of good moral character in this town – (cries of 'No, No' and laughter)'.[26]

These cases epitomize the relationship between local and central authorities in Mid-Victorian Scotland: the Parochial Boards were the heirs of the former kirk sessions (there were still Protestant ministers on the Boards in the 1850s and 1860s) and thus, in true Presbyterian tradition, were defiant towards central authority. The Scottish councillors criticized the interventionist attitude of the Board of Supervision whereas the Catholics were eager to get help from central authorities, as James Fraser Gordon, an Edinburgh Catholic magistrate put it in 1850:

> I shall be very sorry indeed to find that the Board of Supervision, – to which the country looks with the utmost confidence for protection from such proceedings at the instance of local Boards, – is not invested with the necessary power to put an effectual check to such an act as that which has just been perpetrated.[27]

In January 1879 the new buildings hosting the Greenock Parochial Board were inaugurated and the names of Neil Brown and Charles Carbery, both Catholic members, were engraved along with the other 30 members of the Management Committee.[28] This bore testimony to the stable Irish Catholic participation in parochial affairs. In time, Catholic members were given key positions.[29] In 1879, during a ceremony celebrating his Monklands career, James McAuley had exposed the 'difficulties he had to combat with when first he became a member... And now, he said, at the Parochial Board the Catholics received fair play, honour and honesty'.[30] Once they were established in parochial affairs, Irish members did not always adopt a united front concerning local decisions. For instance, in 1893, Samuel Kilpatrick and George Montague argued on the issue of distributing coal to the city's deserving poor.[31] Kilpatrick proposed a motion in favour of the distribution, while Montague reminded his colleague that the Inspector of Poor had declared such practice illegal. The two men quarrelled, and Kilpatrick declared that 'a man like Mr Montague, who stood on a Tory platform at one time and a Nationalist

DOI: 10.1057/9781137329844

platform at another' was in no position to argue.[32] After several bitter remarks had been exchanged, a Scottish member, McLellan had to stop the fight by saying: 'we don't want any washing of dirty linen here'.

The 1894 Local Government Act instituted new elected Parish Councils which dealt, as their predecessors had done, with poverty and sanitation. The voting system was based on the single vote (as opposed to the cumulative vote for School Boards) and the Irish Catholics were scrupulously prepared for the first elections in 1895. In Greenock, the two newly elected Catholic members, Robert Cook and Neil Haughey, were respectively nominated chairman of the Relief Committee and vice-chairman of the Poorhouse Committee.[33] The New Monkland Parish Council elections showed the existing 'friendship of the two sects' (Catholics and Protestants), with one of the Catholic candidates, Patrick McGeehan, who had ten Scottish Protestants on his election committee.[34]

Were municipal councils impregnable strongholds?

During the mid-Victorian era, the Irish were somehow 'excluded' from municipal councils, although they did play a role in town council elections. Thus, in 1862, a unique testimony revealed the Catholics' *modus operandi* in Airdrie:

> our mode of action in Airdrie, which has generally been successful in excluding from our Council Board all who are adverse to our creed and race. We, some 15 years ago, adopted the two following resolutions: – First, That in all elections we never pledge ourselves to support any candidate until we, the Catholic electors, hold a meeting, where the merits and demerits of each candidate is brought forward, and the best men selected. Second, that as we elect four councillors annually, we will at least be unanimous for three men leaving each of us the power of voting for whom we please for the fourth. The political parties are so equally balanced with us, that although we number only about 25 electors, we by our united action have often put in our friends and expelled our enemies.[35]

Surviving Airdrie municipal poll books (1861–67) give us an interesting insight into the political behaviour of different local Irishmen. Throughout this six-year period, the choices of at least five local prominent Irishmen (out of the claimed 25 voters) that could be identified have been examined.[36] The analysis of the poll books reveals that, as a

DOI: 10.1057/9781137329844

rule, the Irish went together to the polling station, at the same time of day, and their choices, if different, varied in the selection of one or two men at the most. The Irishmen voted both for Conservative and Liberal candidates, but their choices might differ: two Irishmen generally represented opposite tendencies, namely James McAuley (Liberal) and John Lavelle (Conservative).[37] Nevertheless, voting patterns changed from one election to another: for example, in 1861, all Irishmen but John Lavelle voted for three Liberal candidates and another who was 'the publicans' candidate' (Mr Black) whereas John Lavelle voted for one Liberal and two Conservative nominees.[38] Another controversy divided the Irish Catholic electors in 1862: at the Catholic meeting preceding the municipal elections, 15 members had promised to vote for Matthew Thom, a Liberal slater. Notwithstanding, on the way to the polling station, the Tory committee managed to convince four of the latter to vote for Conservatives candidates.[39] This affair led to a heated correspondence published in the *Free Press*. Each party accused the other of corruption, and some argued that they had not voted for Thom as he 'had opposed the admission of Roman Catholics on the Parochial Board'.[40] In turn, this led Thom to answer these charges in the same newspaper: 'I always believed and still adhere to that belief that Catholics are entitled, as a matter of right, to a fair representation at the Parochial Board'.[41] A few years later, in 1865, Airdrie Irishmen selected two Tory and two Liberal contestants.[42] In local elections, personal friendship and business relations played a greater role than political beliefs.

Some bold Irishmen, like James McAuley of Airdrie, contested municipal elections in the late 1860s: in 1868, the former schoolmaster (now a publican) was a Liberal candidate. With 496 votes, he came last in the poll.[43] In Greenock, Charles Carbery, an Irish candidate to the Water Trust election in 1864, strongly irritated Scottish opinion. Taking up arms against him, three Scottish candidates published a pamphlet in which their Catholic opponent was labelled as a 'Popish Trustee' and a 'rank Romanist'.[44] The pamphlet was violently anti-Catholic, but was also innovative in that the Irish-Scottish quarrel within the Catholic Church was used against Catholics as an electoral argument – the authors implied that the Catholics were incapable of administering themselves, and therefore could not be trusted 'to take part in our Local government'. The penmen also called to mind Greenock's sectarian history: the pamphlet mentioned James Danaher who was the Irish resident priest during the 1850s anti-Catholic riots; whereas William Gordon, who was the

DOI: 10.1057/9781137329844

vicar of Saint Mary's when the pamphlet was written, was protected on account of his Scottishness ('gentlemanly, mild and clever'). In spite of the violence of the attack, Carbery managed, after a 'lively and exciting contest', to come second in the poll.[45]

Contesting the municipal elections in Greenock was in fact an arduous task for ambitious local Irishmen. Although some did manage to get elected to the Greenock Police Board, only one of them (Robert Cook) succeeded in gaining access to the Town Council. Sectarianism and lack of Catholic mobilization explained unsuccessful Irish municipal bids. In 1890, Brighton opposed his Catholic rival, Robert Cook, in the sixth ward and circulated leaflets directing to vote for 'John Brighton, the Protestant candidate'.[46] As a rule, Catholics running for municipal elections were often looked upon as 'intruders' by their Scottish counterparts. The 'kirkin' o' the town council' affair in 1896 Greenock proved how far Scotsmen equated Scottishness with Presbyterianism. In November 1896, Provost Elskine, the newly appointed mayor, proposed a motion that this churching custom be abandoned, yet some councillors strongly protested against it, arguing that 'the history of Scotland was associated with the Church' – another member, Swan, adding that 'the councillors, as the public representatives of the town, should maintain the good old custom of going to church in a body and show their appreciation for the Presbyterian form of government in this country'.[47] Thus, exercising local power was deeply associated with the democratic form of Presbyterianism – and deeply antagonistic to imagined or real Catholic visions of power. Irish Catholics resented this Scottish attitude, as George Montague expressed it in 1894: 'though I am free to confess that religious and racial prejudice are largely on the decline, still the palpable fact remains that only one gentleman of that communion has been able under the ward system to penetrate the sacred precincts of the Town Council'.[48]

In 1885, Coatbridge acquired burgh status, and thus was to be administered by an elected Town Council, a new institution which local Irish elites were fast to conquer. In November 1885, the first municipal elections were held, and out of a total of 15 councillors, three Irish Catholics were victorious, namely Henry Bannen (who topped the poll in the third ward and was appointed Baillie), Hugh O'Hear and John Lavelle.[49] Several factors accounted for Irish Catholic electoral success: first, the 1884–85 electoral reforms had bettered the working class Irish's access to voting; second, by the mid-1880s, local Irish elites had a dense parochial

DOI: 10.1057/9781137329844

and parliamentary electoral network, which they made use of for their municipal campaigns. By contrast, the Airdrie Town Council, which had existed since the 1830s, had to wait until 1887 to see its first Catholic councillor (of Irish descent), Alexander McKillop, a School Board member, win a seat.[50]

Temperance, Orangemen and Clergymen

The issue of temperance became instrumental when it came to combining religion and local politics. There was certainly a clear distinction between the Catholic vision of temperance as moderation and the Protestant definition of temperance as sheer abstinence. The temperance issue could thus be used as a means of debarring Irish publicans from local honours. It also provoked divisions within the Catholic community. From the 1870s, the Orange Lodges, advocates of the Temperance cause, emerged as new political partners for their Scottish Protestant counterparts in elections. For example, in November 1874, Orangemen took an active part in the Greenock Police Board election campaign against Neil Brown, the Catholic publican candidate. The press reported that 'Tuesday's election was not fought on political grounds, but on religious and temperance principles – Protestantism and total abstinence versus Roman Catholicism and the liquor traffic'.[51] Furthermore, in 1884, ex-Provost Campbell was defeated in his own municipal ward because he was 'strongly opposed by the Orange party, which he considered was not right, as it introduced to their local politics features that had hitherto been awaiting'.[52] In the Monklands, Orangemen started an independent organization to designate their own local candidates. An 1890 press report stated that the Coatbridge District Loyal Orange Lodge (No.22) had resolved to appoint an electoral committee to take part in national and local elections.[53] In 1895, the same lodge decided to run two candidates in the Old Monkland Parish Elections, one of whom, John Stewart Bell, was a 25-year-old Irish-born coal miner.[54] Moreover, Irish Protestant ministers did take an interest in municipal affairs. Such was the case of the Reverend William Harris Winter, from County Sligo, who took charge of the Episcopalian parish of Saint Paul's (Coatbridge) in 1895. As District Chaplain of the Orange Order and President of the Coatbridge Ministers' Temperance Association (in 1898), he was a well-known figure amongst Irish Protestants.[55] In 1900, he headed a delegation

DOI: 10.1057/9781137329844

sent to the Old Monkland School Board, objecting to a Roman Catholic being nominated in place of a late Catholic member. The deputation brought to the board a memorial signed by 1150 electors, but it failed in its request, as Arthur Malone, a familiar figure of Irish Catholic politics was elected in place of the late Father Hughes.

The influence exercised by Catholic clergymen in all aspects of Irish Catholic life (in spiritual as well as political matters) has been described by W. M. Walker as dictatorial.[56] However, in the three towns, Catholic clergymen did not really fit into this profile or rather, Walker probably underestimated the Catholic population's resistance to overbearing priests.

In Greenock, Catholic resistance to what could appear as clerical domination was praised by Scottish citizens. This was the case with Robert Cook, a Catholic pawnbroker, League of the Cross member and active Liberal and Nationalist. Cook's relationship with the local clergy had not been without tension, and when he ran as a municipal candidate in the fifth ward in 1882, the local newspaper argued that he had 'entered the School Board against the strongly pronounced wishes of the late Dean Gordon and the present parish priest, Rev. Alex Taylor.'[57] For Protestant electors who supported him, it was 'meritorious for a Catholic to be rebellious and insubordinate to his ecclesiastic superiors.'[58]

Overall, Catholic priests in Airdrie and Coatbridge could not be accused of dictating votes to their parishioners. There were, however, exceptions, such as Father John Hughes, who served as an assistant priest in Saint Margaret's, Airdrie (1877–83) and as a parish priest in Saint Augustine's Church, Coatbridge from 1892.[59] This Irish clergyman was very charismatic and had a natural gift for politics for 'at School, Parochial and Parliamentary elections he was a force to be reckoned with.'[60] In the 1892 Coatbridge Town Council elections, Father Hughes and his 'Temperance Party' gave their support to two Protestant candidates, Mr Dick and Mr Fleming, in the third and fifth wards of Coatbridge, who were running against two prominent Irish Catholics spirit dealers (Charles O'Neill and John Lavelle). This led to the defeat of O'Neill in the third ward by only 39 votes, to the candidate's great dismay: 'I had so far succeeded in establishing my position with the Protestant electors in the ward that I had every title to anticipate success had it not been for the grossly unfair and totally unexplainable conduct of Fr Hughes in connection with the election.'[61] What seemed even more unjust to the unfortunate Irish candidate was that Mr Dick was not a professed

DOI: 10.1057/9781137329844

teetotaller, and was supported by the priest only to oppose the spirit dealer. John Lavelle, the other Irish candidate, managed to secure his seat, but he was reported to have called Father's Hughes attitude 'clerical dictation'. Father Hughes supported his own Roman Catholic candidate in this election, Charles Quinn, an Irish Catholic teetotaller, who lost against Mr Smellie, the Protestant candidate.

Not only did Father Hughes' anger lay Catholics, he also entered into conflict with fellow priests. At the Old Monkland Parish Elections of 1895, he encouraged John Cooper, an engineman, to contest the fourth ward, where Father Curran (of Saint Mary's, Whifflet) was already a candidate.[62] In Charles O'Neill's opinion, the running of two Roman Catholic candidates for this ward divided the votes and resulted in no Catholic being elected at all.[63] Father Hughes' attitude in local elections caused his fellow priests to be very upset. In 1897, Canon McCay, of Saint Patrick's (Coatbridge) nearly resigned because of Father Hughes' behaviour. He wrote to the Archbishop: 'my opinion of Father Hughes' conduct at recent municipal elections, and former ones… to him was due on that occasion the defeat of the Catholic candidate by a Protestant'.[64] Canon McCay was referring both to the 1897 School board elections in Coatbridge, where Father Hughes brought forward a miners' agent, John Donaldson, against the wishes of the other local priests and the Vicar General, Dr Maguire. In November that year, at the Town Council elections, Father Hughes chose not to support Bailie Benson, the Irish Catholic spirit merchant seeking re-election (a 'universally popular' figure amongst Protestants and Catholics) in the fourth ward (Benson stood against Mr Arnott, a Scottish spirit merchant).[65] Father Hughes proclaimed that he was going to abstain from voting for either of the two men, and 'made a house to house visitation of the Catholic electors in his division of the ward'.[66] An interesting insight into Father Hughes' canvassing methods had been given on a former occasion (1894), when he remained all day at the entrance of the polling station, throwing 'abusive and insulting epithets to all he suspected to be voting for Benson [the Catholic spirit merchant candidate]'.[67] Thus this 'Modern Father Mathew' managed to anger his fellow priests and parishioners (even the very temperate and faithful Catholic Charles O'Neill described him as 'tyrannical and overbearing', and as a 'Demon of discord'). This exceptional case was linked to the strong personality and charisma of Father Hughes: overall, if parish priests did have an influence in local elections in the Monklands, their role could not be generally described as dictatorial.

DOI: 10.1057/9781137329844

The very fact that Father Hughes' attitude caused such chaos in the Irish Catholic community is the ultimate proof that not all priests behaved in this authoritative way.[68]

The Irish and local politics during the Edwardian era

In 1903, the Catholic *Glasgow Examiner* boasted: 'In the Town Boards we have representatives; a large number of gentlemen have been placed on the Justices of the Peace roll.'[69] To a certain extent, this optimistic perspective mirrored a real increase in Irish participation on local boards. The first change to take place in the early twentieth century was the renewal of Irish local political generations. Irish figures of standing, such as Daniel Carlin or Henry Bannen in the Monklands and Daniel McLaughlin in Greenock died in their sixties.[70] When Carlin, a native of Donegal, passed away in December 1906, the Airdrie newspaper reported that 'his death remove[d] another of the few remaining links with the Airdrie of nearly half a century ago'.[71] Carlin had been a member of the New Monkland Parish Council since the 1850s, as well as a Court House commissioner.[72] Several months later, Henry Bannen, who had emigrated from Roscommon to Coatbridge in his childhood, died at his Coatbridge home.[73] He had directed Saint Margaret schools from 1869 to 1895, and he won the first municipal elections in 1885, thus becoming 'the second Catholic Bailie who had occupied this position in Scotland'.[74]

The younger Irish political generation that arose during the Edwardian period did not have to fight as their forefathers had; they were also more preoccupied with Scottish issues and involved in British movements such as trade unionism and Labour. In the Monklands, Patrick Agnew symbolized this new generation: he was born of Irish parentage, and as well as being an active Catholic and an executive member of the Irish National Foresters, he was also a leading Trade Unionist (one of the Miners County Executive leaders in 1896). He was elected to the Coatbridge Town Council in 1911 as the first ever official Labour candidate.[75] In Greenock, Neil Haughey was another icon of this new generation of local political leaders: hailing from Ulster, he entered the Greenock municipal arena in the late 1890s (when elected Parish Councillor in 1895).[76] Without his being affiliated to Labour, he used his trade union activities as a political reference. He was famed for his witty eloquence – as for instance when, in February 1912, he pleaded at the Parish Council for the use of butter

DOI: 10.1057/9781137329844

instead of margarine in the Poorhouse. Robert Burns' poetry was his main argument:

> He liked to see Burns' works admired, but he would also like to see his principles acted upon. 'Man's inhumanity to man makes countless thousands mourn'... 'When man to man, the world o'er, Shall brithers be, for a' that'.[77]

Irish Catholic representation on Parish Councils was nonetheless still in jeopardy. For example, in 1901 the Greenock press protested against the fact that six Catholic candidates were running because: 'Neither by reason of tax-paying, nor population, nor ownership of property in the burgh, are they entitled to have six members on the Council, though unfortunately the proportion of their people at Smithton, not to speak of the outdoor poor, is too large.'[78] George Montague, one of the Irish Catholic candidates, reacted to this rise of the 'well nigh dead spirit of religious bigotry'.[79] However, this Protestant discontent, combined with Catholic electoral apathy and division, resulted in the defeat of all six Catholic candidates.[80] Thus, sectarianism had not disappeared from local elections – in 1902, George Montague tried to have Catholics nominated on two vacant municipal seats, protesting against 'narrow-minded bigots who have gone back 50 years for a war cry at election that used to adorn every corner in those old bad days, to wit, No Irish need apply'.[81] Although the Irish Catholics' participation on Parish Boards seemed more secure in the Monklands, Scottish Protestant opposition could still emerge during electoral campaigns.[82] For instance, in 1910, Old Monkland Parish Council Scottish candidates received a letter from the Old Monkland Protestant Vigilance Association asking:

1 Have you, in connection with this Parish Council Election, at any time solicited the assistance of the Roman Catholic priest, or of the organizations of the Roman Catholic Church?

2 In the event of being returned, will you make inquiry as to the causes of the great preponderance of the Roman Catholic paupers... [who have a] claim upon the parochial funds?[83]

Irish Catholic interests on local boards were definitely broader than what they had been in the late Victorian era.[84] On municipal boards, issues such as lighting, public hygiene and policing did not result in sectarian or religious divisions, and at first sight, Irish members acted according to their political beliefs, whether inspired by Liberal or Conservative ideas. For example, in January 1914, Patrick Agnew and Charles O'Neill voted

DOI: 10.1057/9781137329844

in favour of the municipalization of the local gas company, whereas John Lavelle opposed the motion.[85] However, sectarian tensions were perceptible on certain occasions, and in the Coatbridge Town Council the 'burgh organist affair' provoked disputes between 1911 and 1914. In May 1911, the Town Council (with a majority of seven votes against four) had appointed Patrick O'Neill, a Catholic second-generation Irishman, who taught at Saint Patrick's school, as the burgh organist.[86] The local press suspected that Established Church councillors had preferred to nominate a Catholic rather than a Dissenter for this position.[87] This appointment was continuously disputed between hard-line Protestants and their Catholic and Liberal colleagues. When in April 1913, Smith, one of the councillors, suggested that O'Neill's contract be rescinded, Patrick Agnew exclaimed that 'in the administration of the laws of a city, there should be no favour shown to colour, creed or class'.[88] When in 1914, the Baptist councillor Samuel Lindsay tried to fire O'Neill, judge Liddle fought him back arguing that 'In their public works they had Catholics and Protestants working together in perfect harmony... It was simply a case of religious persecution and bigotry.'[89] John Lavelle, one of the Irish Catholic members further added that: 'Mr Patrick O'Neill – he might put it plainly – was the only Catholic official employed in this burgh and for that reason that discussion always took place.'[90]

By 1914, Irish Catholic representation on the municipal board was still wanting in Greenock. Two factors explained the Irish Catholic lack of enthusiasm for the Greenock Town Council. First, the financial cost of a municipal campaign was a major constraint for local Irish elites, who also had to incur the expense of Parish Council elections campaigns.[91] Second, the politicization of municipal elections did not have a positive effect on Irish nationalists campaigning since Liberal and Conservative clubs sometimes paid for their candidates' expenses in local elections, whereas the United Irish League did not.

Conclusion

The Irish in the Monklands and in Greenock were eager to participate in local politics as early as the 1850s. Their involvement was not restricted solely to an Irish local élite, as the nomination and election of active members had to be supported by the majority of Irish voters, no matter how small their numbers were at first.

DOI: 10.1057/9781137329844

The examination of this too-long-neglected aspect of Irish political life in Scotland has demonstrated how local issues could both unite and divide Irish communities. The traditional view of a united Irish Catholic front in political matters is, in fact, far from accurate. Yet, while plagued by internal divisions, the Irish fully partook in local self-administration, a major feature of Scottish identity.

Notes

1   M. Atkinson (1904) *Local Government in Scotland* (Edinburgh), pp. 7–10.
2   T.M. Devine (2000) *The Scottish Nation 1700-2000* (London: Penguin), p. 287.
3   *FP*, 16 August 1852.
4   *GH*, 21 August 1868.
5   *GA*, 29 April 1868.
6   *FP*, 5 December 1863.
7   *GA*, 19 March 1852. The 'test' mentioned was the 'poorhouse test', whereby certain poor relief applicants were offered the poorhouse in the first place (mainly the elderly, single mothers and ill people) – if they refused, they were denied assistance.
8   PP, 1868–1869 (301) XI.1301: *Report from the Select Committee on Poor Law (Scotland)*, p. 325.
9   *GA*, 17 June 1882.
10   *GA*, 17 June 1882.
11   *GA*, 26 August 1882.
12   *FP*, 3 March 1860.
13   PP, 1870 (357) XI.1: *Report from the Select Committee on Poor Law (Scotland)*, p. 208.
14   *GH*, 29 April 1868.
15   *GO*, 17 October 1896.
16   PP, 1863 (518) LII.519: Copy of any Regulations, Instructions or Correspondence of the Board of Supervision in Scotland relating to Religious Instruction of the Pauper Children of Roman Catholic Parents.
17   PP, 1863 (518) LII.519: 'That all the children who are inmates of the Poorhouse be brought up in the religious persuasion of the majority of the heritors and ratepayers of the community'.
18   PP, 1863 (518) LII.519: Letter from James Danaher to J. F. Gordon, 2 September 1850: 'We dissent from the decision...: first, That it is an attempt to proselytise the Roman Catholic children; and second, it is not warranted by the rules sent from the Board of Supervision fort he guidance of the poorhouse of Greenock'.

DOI: 10.1057/9781137329844

19　PP, 1863 (518) LII.519: Letter from Inspector of Poor to Board of Supervision, 9 September 1850.

20　PP, 1863 (518) LII.519: From Board of Supervision to Inspector of Poor, 11 September 1850.

21　*The Glasgow Sentinel*, 23 November 1850.

22　*FP*, 20 December 1862.

23　PP, 1863 (518) LII.519.

24　PP, 1863 (518) LII.519 : Letter from Archibald Gerald, of Rochsoles, to Board of Supervision, 11 June 1853.

25　*GA*, 27 September 1882.

26　*GA*, 29 September 1882.

27　SCA, SM/13/14: Robert Campbell, Esq. (1863) *Past and Present treatment of Roman Catholic Children in Scotland by the Board of Supervision*, p. 3.

28　*GA*, 29 January 1879.

29　In 1887, Patrick Colligan was chairman of the Relief Committee and Samuel Kilpatrick was vice-chairman of the Accounts Committee on the Greenock Parochial Board (*GT*, 30 March 1887).

30　*AC*, 29 May 1881.

31　*GT*, 1 February 1893.

32　*GT*, 1 February 1893.

33　*GT*, 17 May 1895.

34　*GO*, 30 March 1895.

35　*AC*, 4 October 1862.

36　*AC*, 4 October 1862; NLA, UA/1/11/2/3: *Airdrie poll register detailing elections of councillors* (1861–1867). The Irishmen identified were: James McAuley; Daniel Carlin; Michael McKillop, pawnbroker (father of Alexander McKillop); John Lavell, pawnbroker; Charles McGeechan, grocer and Francis McKearney, spirit dealer.

37　*AC*, 4 October 1862.

38　*AC*, 25 October 1862; NLA, UA/1/11/2/3: Airdrie Municipal election, 5 November 1861.

39　*FP*, 22 October 1862.

40　*FP*, 29 November 1862.

41　*FP*, 6 December 1862.

42　NLA, UA/1/11/2/3: Airdrie Municipal Election, 7 November 1865.

43　*AC*, 5 December 1868.

44　SCA, DD2/39/12: Condon papers, poster (*circa* November 1864). See Appendix 2.

45　*FP*, 12 November 1864.

46　*GT*, 4 November 1890.

47　*GT*, 7 November 1896.

48　*GT*, 25 September 1894.

DOI: 10.1057/9781137329844

49   *CE*, 4 November 1885.

50   *CE*, 22 November 1887.

51   *GA*, 12 November 1874.

52   *GA*, 8 November 1882. Evidently, these 'features' had manifested themselves before 1884.

53   *AC*, 15 November 1890.

54   *CE*, 6 February 1895; *1891 Census: Old Monkland*, 652/2, Enumeration District no. 35.

55   *CE*, 25 September 1895; 6 December 1899.

56   W. Walker (1972) 'Irish Immigrants in Scotland Their Priests, Politics and Parochial Life', *The Historical Journal*, XV, p. 659. Priests are compared with Communist Party secretaries in the USSR, in terms of parochial organizations.

57   *GA*, 10 April 1879.

58   *GA*, 6 November 1882; *GA*, 27 March 1879.

59   See for example a 'Meeting of Roman Catholics' chaired by Fr McIntosh in Saint Margaret's Schoolroom, Airdrie. For the coming municipal elections, the priest recommended 'Mr Deedes [a Conservative] as a fit and proper person to represent them', but his motion 'fell to the ground' (*AC*, 30 October 1869).

60   *CE*, 15 August 1900.

61   GAA, GC 29/95: Letter from Charles O'Neill to Archbishop Eyre, 12 December 1897.

62   GAA, GC 29/95: Letter from Charles O'Neill, 12 December 1897.

63   GAA, GC 29/95: Letter from Charles O'Neill, 12 December 1897.

64   GAA, GC 29/14: Letter from Canon McCay to Archbishop Eyre, 6 December 1897.

65   GAA, GC 29/95: Letter from Charles O'Neill, 12 December 1897.

66   GAA, GC 29/95: Letter from Charles O'Neill, 12 December 1897.

67   GAA, GC 29/95: Letter from Charles O'Neill, 12 December 1897.

68   J. McCaffrey (1978) 'Politics and the Catholic Community Since 1878', *Innes Review*, 29, p. 144.

69   *GE*, 3 January 1903.

70   *GT*, 17 November 1904.

71   *AC*, 5 January 1907.

72   *CE*, 2 January 1907.

73   *AC*, 21 December 1907.

74   *AC*, 21 December 1907.

75   A. McDonagh (nd.) 'Irish Immigrants and Labour Movements in Coatbridge and Airdrie, 1891–1931', B.A. Honours Dissertation, University of Strathclyde, p. 83.

76   *GT*, 3 April 1895.

DOI: 10.1057/9781137329844

77   *GT*, 28 February 1912.
78   *GT*, 24 October 1901.
79   *GT*, 25 October 1901.
80   *GT*, 4 November 1901.
81   *GT*, 8 August 1902.
82   *GE*, 9 November 1901.
83   *CL*, 29 October 1910.
84   *GT*, 28 August 1901.
85   *CL*, 17 January 1914.
86   *AC*, 3 June 1911.
87   *CE*, 24 May 1911.
88   *CL*, 19 April 1913.
89   *CL*, 19 April 1914.
90   *CL*, 19 April 1914.
91   Neil Haughey explained before an electoral audience that his expenses were paid 'out of his own pocket, as he had done at previous elections' (*GT*, 1 November 1912).

DOI: 10.1057/9781137329844

6
National(ist) Issues

Abstract: *Chapter 6 examines the national dimension of Irish political involvement both before and after the passing of the 1868 and 1884–85 suffrage reform acts. It contributes to the wider picture of the Irish nationalist vote in Britain by demonstrating that Irish political organization was already well-entrenched as early as the 1850s (in contrast with the small number of potential Irish voters) and that in the Monklands (particularly in Coatbridge), the Irish Nationalist movement became highly influential. Locally, the Liberal candidates had to come to terms with Irish nationalist electors, especially after the 1880s electoral reforms. The chapter also explores the divisions within the Irish nationalist community during electoral campaigns.*

Vaughan, Geraldine. *The 'Local' Irish in the West of Scotland, 1851–1921*. Basingstoke: Palgrave Macmillan, 2013. DOI: 10.1057/9781137329844.

As Donald MacRaild has argued, in line with contemporary historiography, 'the Irish in Britain were important participants in the movements that shaped both Irish and British working-class political culture over the nineteenth century.'[1] Yet the Irish migrants' involvement in national politics was limited prior to 1868 because of their restricted access to suffrage. Their partaking in 'physical force' nationalism has been uncovered by several studies. The Irish Republican Brotherhood (IRB) recruited members in Scottish Western towns. For instance, Charles O'Neill, the local Irish nationalist leader, made no mystery of his past Glaswegian Fenian activities in the 1860s. Yet, by the 1870s, the Fenian movement was winding down, and constitutional aspirations became the major driving political force.

Physical force nationalism

In his recent study of physical force Irish republicanism, Máirtín Ò Catháin stressed the century-long connection between Irish 'rebels' and Scotland – which went back to the incoming of United Irishmen in the wake of the failed '98 attempt.[2] During the mid-Victorian era, Fenians, or members of the Irish Republican Brotherhood (IRB), were the most influential armed movement within the Irish diaspora. But how did this impact Western Scottish towns? Ò Catháin calculated that a total 8,000 IRB members were active in Scotland, and Elaine McFarland had previously estimated that 2,500 Fenians were active in Glasgow and its surroundings in the 1860s.[3] As regards the Monklands and Greenock, it is difficult to ascertain the actual figures of a membership in an underground movement. Local press reports seem to have been keen on exaggerating Fenian presence – in 1865, some witnesses swore that they had seen 900 men (aged between 20 and 40) drilling at night on the outskirts of town.[4] In the Monklands, an 1867 press report stated that a group of Coatbridge Irish workers had left town to join a rebellion attempt in Ireland. Eight of them were arrested and imprisoned in Sligo – this led the journalist to conclude that '[they] ha[d] a sprinkling of the Fenian Brotherhood still amongst us, and from the fact that private meetings have been held weekly, in houses suspected to have a tender regard for the green, shows that a lodge, if not lodges, exist in our locality'.[5] One branch of the IRB must have existed in Airdrie, for in 1864 the local priest, Duncan McNab, denounced three supposed members

DOI: 10.1057/9781137329844

of the organisation during mass, including James McAuley.[6] In fact, the greatest impact of Fenianism in the three Western towns under study was probably, as argued by McFarland, more cultural, psychological and related to identity issues. The word *Fenian*, past the 'Fenian panic' in the late 1860s, became a way of potentially designating any Irish nationalist. At the height of the 'Fenian panic' in 1867, the editor of *The Airdrie and Coatbridge Advertiser* wrote that 'now Irishman means Fenian…We have received them amongst us with hospitality… A tide of adverse feeling is rising throughout the country'.[7]

The growth of the constitutional nationalist movement

The constitutional nationalist movement really took off in Scotland in the early 1870s. In December 1871, John Ferguson launched the Glasgow Home Rule Association – which was federated with other British branches into the Home Rule Confederation of Great Britain (HRCGB) in January 1873.[8] Nevertheless, at a local level, Irish nationalists had started to organise since the 1860s. Individual figures emerged in the Monklands – such as James McAuley, the Airdrie former schoolteacher and publican, who launched an O'Connell fund with Michael McKillop and John Devlin in January 1855. McAuley regularly attended Liberal and Conservative meetings during parliamentary campaigns and was to be found heckling candidates on Irish Catholic issues such as the Maynooth grant or proposed governmental inspections of convents and monasteries.[9] In Greenock, the Greenock Irish National Association was founded in 1865.[10]

Amongst middle-sized Western Scottish towns, Coatbridge emerged as a key nationalist city, where major Irish rallies were organized in the 1870s and 1880s. Charismatic Irish local leaders, such as James McAuley and Charles O'Neill, greatly contributed to Coatbridge's leading position. O'Neill was first a member of the IRB in the late 1860s, and he became one of the key organizers of the Home Rule movement in the West of Scotland along with John Ferguson. The HRCGB gave way to the founding of the Land League as the 'land war' broke out in Ireland in 1879. Its founder, Michael Davitt, who had emigrated to Lancashire in 1851, acted as secretary for the IRB in 1868 and was imprisoned from 1870 to 1877. In March 1881, the Coatbridge section of the Irish National

DOI: 10.1057/9781137329844

Land League (ILL) was inaugurated. The foundation of the ILL reflected an attempt at reconciling constitutional and revolutionary nationalism.[11] Yet the replacement of the Land League by the Irish National League of Great Britain (INL) in 1882, under Parnellite leadership, demonstrated a will to concentrate on Westminster politics. The development of INL branches in Scotland was impressive: by 1890 there were 630 branches and 40,000 members countrywide.[12] In April 1890, the Irish National League in Coatbridge had 900 members, and was considered as 'the Premier Branch of Great-Britain'.[13] In Airdrie, the Daniel O'Connell section was created in 1888, but was suspended momentarily in 1897 because of financial problems.[14]

By the late 1870s, Greenock seemed to lag behind the Monklands in terms of nationalist organization. In June 1877, an Irish reader wrote to the local press about the lack of Irish enthusiasm: the absence of 'reading-rooms, electoral associations, lecture halls, social clubs, private educational classes' leading to a lack of 'cohesion amongst them, no preparedness for the time of battle'.[15] During the 1877 legislative electoral campaign, John Ferguson had bills posted in town encouraging the 'Irishmen of Greenock' to be 'firm and decisive' and 'strike a blow that will at once and forever place you in Greenock on a political platform to command respect'.[16] Although there was no branch of the Home Rule Confederation in Greenock, the Land League started to develop early in the 1880s. Nevertheless, local authorities could, at times, hinder the League's progress. For instance, in 1882, the executive committee of the local INL requested the use of a harbour shed for the visit of Michael Davitt (because the Town Hall was undergoing repairs). This application provoked a debate within the Harbour Trust, and councillor Maceachran, citing Davitt's Fenian past, even challenged the legality of such a gathering.[17] Nonetheless, the League expanded and several local sections were created, of which, however, the John Dillon Branch was the only one to exist continuously until 1900. Amongst its executives were the main local Irish figures, including Neil Haughey, a stationer, George Montague, a newsagent, John McGiveran, a tailor, and Patrick and Samuel Fitzpatrick, both publicans.

Tensions within the local branches of the League mirrored dissensions within the Irish nationalist movement in Britain at large. In 1890, the Monklands sections at first unanimously approved of Parnell's condemnation over his divorce scandal – thus following the anti-Parnellite move of most Scottish branches.[18] However, in April 1891, a group of Irishmen led by

DOI: 10.1057/9781137329844

Bernard Dorris, a former INL executive, launched the Coatbridge Parnell Leadership Committee.[19] A few months later, it was opposed by the anti-Parnell INL section who described the former as a 'snake-like' faction.[20] In 1895, the Parnell Committee supported the Irish National Amnesty Association whose leadership was clergy-dominated. These internal Irish quarrels in Scotland were also (re)exported to Ireland – this was the case when Charles O'Neill, who ran for the South Armagh seat in 1900, was defeated partly as a result of the actions of pro-Healy agitators in Coatbridge, among whom Oswald Hannaway, who had anti-O'Neill pamphlets signed by 'The Coatbridge Irishmen' circulated in the constituency.[21]

In addition to forming local Irish leagues, the Irish nationalists in Scottish cities became familiar with national politics through the development of local parliamentary associations, that is, 'independent debating societies run on the same lines as Parliament, with a 'Government' and 'Opposition, motions and bills'.[22] In 1895, there were five Greenock Irish nationalists amongst 58 members in total.[23] This type of organization encouraged contacts between Nationalists and Liberals, and also between nationalists and the Greenock Radical Association (Robert Cook and James Slavin, both Land Leaguers were members of the Association's executive).[24]

The reunification of the Irish Nationalist Party was effective in 1901 when William O'Brien (1852–1928) took the lead over the new Irish Parliamentary Party (IPP). The Irish National League became the United Irish League (UIL) and from 1900 onwards, the local branches of the INL in the West of Scotland were merged into the UIL. Coatbridge was still to the fore: in 1901, the Michael Davitt UIL section was 'the finest branch in Great Britain', and its chairman, O'Neill, was appointed as one of the three delegates to represent Scottish branches at the 1903 annual conference of the UIL in Liverpool.[25] At the same time, the John Dillon section in Greenock inaugurated a new 900-seat hall, and Neil Haughey, its chairman, declared that: 'in point of proper accommodation they were far ahead of either the local Liberals or the local Conservatives'.[26]

The coronation of Edward VII put the League's authority to the test: since the Coronation Oath was considered injurious and blasphemous for the Irish Catholic subjects, the UIL instructed its members to boycott the various Coronation ceremonies and festivities.[27] The O'Connell branch in Airdrie adopted the following motion in June 1902:

> call on the Irish people of Airdrie and district to refrain from taking any
> part in the forthcoming Coronation celebration and that we exhort all Irish

DOI: 10.1057/9781137329844

parents to prevent their children taking any present in connection with the same, whether in the shape of tin medals or chocolate boxes.[28]

In Greenock, the Irish were required by the Nationalists to refrain from all involvement, and James Hargan, a local UIL member was expelled from the Greenock branch for having voted, along with other shopkeepers, for the closing of shops on Coronation Day.[29] When during the same year the Greenock UIL struck out two members, John Clay and Patrick McKenna, for having joined the local Volunteers Force, Scotsmen reacted vehemently to this Nationalist anti-patriotic attitude, stating that it was right 'for an Irishman to associate himself with a force which exists for the protection of the country he gets his bread and butter in'.[30]

In Britain, the participation of priests in the nationalist movement increased during the late Victorian era. MacRaild has convincingly argued that the growing number of clergymen born in Ireland appointed to British parishes, combined with the increasing respectability of constitutional nationalism accounted for that phenomenon.[31] Yet the idea that the Catholic Church encouraged nationalism to keep its parishioners away from the Labour party must be nuanced.[32] As Roy Foster has justly remarked, 'the Church was always suspicious of Home Rule's protestant origins'[33]– clearly, the Catholic hierarchy in Scotland was not always supportive of overtly nationalist clergymen.[34] For instance, the young Father John Dougan, appointed in Coatbridge in 1886, refused to attend an Irish National League meeting hosted by Father Hughes in order to comply with the directives of the Archbishop, as he stated in writing: 'Since His Grace the Archbishop spoke to me on the subject at the examination, I have severed all connection with that body'.[35] The degree of nationalist enthusiasm varied from one priest to another – Scottish priests would generally utter a few words of encouragement if they attended political gatherings, whereas certain Irish priests were highly active. Michael O'Keeffe, of Saint Patrick's (Coatbridge), was nicknamed 'the patriotic priest', and renowned for his nationalist speeches.[36] In October 1885, he chaired an INL meeting with a speech that contained pagan undertones: 'Refuse Home Rule, continue to make Ireland the Niobe of Nations, and there [will] arise a Nemesis to plead for the oppressed people and deal destruction to her enemies.'[37] In July 1886, he stood up during a meeting, crying 'Three cheers for Mr Parnell, the greatest statesman in the world!'[38] Apparently, supporting the nationalist cause was a Coatbridge tradition amongst clergymen, as O'Keeffe put it in 1891 during a ceremony honouring a young priest, McAllister, for his 'carrying out the

DOI: 10.1057/9781137329844

worthy tradition of the priests of Coatbridge who for... half a century have supported the national cause'.[39]

Elections: divided they stood?

'The *raison d'être* of all home rule organisations in Britain', wrote David Fitzpatrick, 'was electoral Branches were required to take "an active part in all parliamentary elections".'[40] As regards Irish voting power, very few Irish immigrants were on the rolls before the Representation of the People (Scotland) Act of 1868. However, the small number of enfranchised did not signify that the Irish voting power was inexistent prior to 1868.[41] In fact, a *Free Press* correspondent explained in 1852 that though there were only 12 Irish electors in Airdrie, 'in a constituency so nicely balanced, where the parliamentary candidate is generally returned by a majority varying from 11 to 30, the votes of 12 or 15 Catholics are not to be despised'.[42] A year later, the Catholic paper encouraged its readers to register:

> This is the period for registration and never could the energetic advice of the late Sir Robert Peel to the electors of England – 'register, register, register'– be more appropriately addressed to the Catholics of Scotland, than at this hour... But how many Catholics in Glasgow, and in other towns and boroughs in Scotland disenfranchise themselves by neglecting to register.[43]

In 1852, two candidates, the Liberal James Merry and James Baird, the Tory local iron manufacturer, fought for the Falkirk constituency (Airdrie). The majority of Irish Catholics agreed, during a meeting, to vote for the Whig candidate. Nevertheless, after the election, John Devlin accused some of them of having failed to respect the agreement. He declared that 'no Catholic could, in conscience, vote for Mr Baird, the supporter of the Ecclesiastical Titles Bill ...and opponent of civil and religious liberty' and thus proposed a vote of censure on the Catholics who had openly supported him (he even mentioned 'canvassing').[44] Local interests were an argument for the Catholics who had supported Baird, the Monklands manufacturer, as Devlin declared:

> They have no better reason to give than that Mr. Baird employs some thirty Catholics in his works at Gartsherrie – has condescended to sell some ground for a Catholic chapel in Coatbridge, and gave (although it is denied) £50 towards its erection... We repeat, that no local considerations could have afforded sufficient justifications for such an act of treachery to the whole Catholic interest.[45]

DOI: 10.1057/9781137329844

In that particular case, it was manifest that local interests prevailed over nationalist beliefs.

The 1868 and 1884–85 suffrage Reform Acts added to the growth of the Irish electorate.[46] Since there were no electoral censuses, it is necessary to rely on the figures given by local Irish nationalist leagues. For instance, in December 1877, the Greenock League declared that there were 700 Irish electors (16 per cent of the total number of electors) and in 1885, it claimed that the number had risen to 1,700 (28 per cent of total).[47] However, while these figures indicated the total number of potential Irish voters, there were numerous would-be electors who failed to register. In June 1888, 300 Irish voters in Greenock were unable to vote because they had forgotten to register.[48] In the Falkirk constituency (Airdrie), the Irish claimed to have 700 electors in 1874, which represented 15 per cent of the electorate.[49]

In Greenock, divisions within the nationalist community were twofold: first, business interests sometimes interfered with nationalist allegiances; second, religious priorities could stand in the way of the ILL's instructions. Local Irish elites were in majority publicans and the Liberal party's stance favouring temperance was resented by spirit dealers. At the same time, Irish publicans were very active within the local sections of the ILL – but when it came to the parliamentary vote they had to choose between their trade's interests and the advancement of the Irish cause. Accordingly, an Irish correspondent wrote to the Greenock Advertiser during the 1878 by-election:

> Is it not a well-known fact that by far the greater majority of those who lay any claim to influence amongst us are publicans? Is it not also a very well-known fact that the Tory candidate is an enemy to the Permissive Bill?[50]

The publicans' opposition to the Liberal Local Option Bill project in 1892 led the Greenock Spirit Trade Association, to which local Irish publicans belonged, to instruct its members to vote for the Unionist

TABLE 6.1   *Members of Parliament for Greenock, 1878–1900*

Parliamentary Elections	Elected MP.	Political Affiliation
1878/1880/1884	James Stewart	Liberal
1884/1885	Thomas Sutherland	Liberal
1886/1892	Thomas Sutherland	Liberal-Unionist
1895	A. E. Fletcher	Liberal
1900	James Reid	Unionist

DOI: 10.1057/9781137329844

candidate, Thomas Sutherland. An Irish reader of the *Greenock Telegraph* reacted against this call to vote for a Conservative candidate:

> Surely this will be a lesson to the men – the working men – who make up the Irish National League of Great-Britain not to place in responsible positions the men whose interests are associated with the party opposed to Home Rule... the 'pot-house' proprietors.[51]

In Greenock, the Catholic Electoral Association clashed with the local Home Rulers in December 1877 and early 1878 – John Ferguson denying the Association the right to instruct Irish voters.[52]

However, matters were smoothed over after Gladstone's conversion to Home Rule, and the ensuing split between Unionists and Liberal Home Rulers. From then on, the INL was in a position to invariably support the Liberals. In 1886, the Greenock INL campaigned for Harold Wilson, the Liberal candidate. After his defeat, the Irish nevertheless thanked 'the Liberal electors of Greenock for supporting the Home Rule candidate, Mr Harold Wilson, at the late Parliamentary election'.[53]

Compared to their counterparts in Greenock, the Monklands Irish were a much more unified community when it came to parliamentary elections. In Airdrie, the Irish nationalist vote went to the candidate in favour of Home Rule, but support could be withdrawn if the candidate was suspected of breaking a promise. This was the case with John Ramsay (Table 6.2), the Liberal candidate for the Falkirk Burghs seat, who received Irish support during the 1874 elections. Yet this endorsement came at a price. In 1880, Ramsay was heckled by the nationalist Alexander McKillop at a public meeting: 'Will Mr Ramsay admit or deny that at the last General Election he received the support of over 600 Catholic electors in the Falkirk Burghs... on the understanding that he would vote for Home Rule in the House of Commons?'[54] Ramsay temporized and answered that he had not pledged to vote for a law that would 'sever the links between Great-Britain and Ireland'.[55] Because of

TABLE 6.2   *Members of Parliament for Falkirk (Airdrie), 1874–1900*

Parliamentary Elections	Elected M.P.	Political Affiliation
1874	John Ramsay	Liberal
1886	William Pirrie Sinclair	Unionist
1892	Harry Smith	Liberal
1895	John Wilson	Unionist

DOI: 10.1057/9781137329844

his ambiguous attitude, the Irish electors withdrew their support from him at the 1886 election.[56]

The Coatbridge Irish nationalist electors, as a rule, faithfully respected the ILL's instructions. In the 1885 parliamentary election, the IPP instructed its voters to vote Tory as part of a reversal of tactics. In Glasgow, John Ferguson opposed the Parnellite manoeuvre and the Liberal candidates were successful.[57] Yet in Coatbridge, the Irish Catholic vote followed the IPP's instructions – for instance, James Lynch, the headmaster of Saint Patrick's school, 'was instrumental in organizing the Nationalist voting power, which contributed so much to the success of the Conservative candidate, John Baird'.[58] When the League ordered to vote Conservative at the 1885 elections, the Irish electors did so. They voted Liberal the following year, according to the INL's national order. Locally, some Irish groups tried to put pressure on Liberal MPs in exchange for their electoral support. For instance, in 1887, Robert Cunnighame Graham, the Liberal MP for Coatbridge, complained of a Catholic association. Graham stated that the association's secretary, Richard Macready, had tried to pressurise him into funding the society by writing: 'our people have a claim on your charity, for they were solely instrumental in rejecting you in 1885 and in returning you in 1886'.[59] Even though the Nationalist–Liberal alliance was strong after Gladstone's conversion to the Irish cause, the Coatbridge's Irish support to the Liberals was always negotiated by the League. For instance, in February 1899, the Nationalists were upset that the Liberals had chosen a candidate without consulting the INL. As John Ferguson exclaimed: 'in a constituency like this, [I deny] the right of the Liberal party to chose a candidate without consulting the Irish nationalists'.[60] After the INL and the Liberal Party had agreed, Douglas was elected and owed his victory to the Irish voters – as Douglas' opponent stated: 'There was one party for which the

TABLE 6.3   *Members of Parliament for North-West Lanarkshire (Coatbridge),*
1878–1900

Parliamentary Election	Elected M.P.	Political Affiliation
1874	Thomas Edward Colebrooke	Liberal
1885	John Baird	Unionist
1886	Robert Cunnighame Graham	Liberal
1892	Alexander Whitelaw	Unionist
1895	John Goundry Holburn	Liberal
1899/1900	Charles Mackinnon Douglas	Liberal

DOI: 10.1057/9781137329844

election in North-West Lanarkshire had been a victory, and that party was the Irish nationalists.'[61]

The Nationalist–Liberal alliance was still strong during the 1906 and 1910 elections. The local UIL branches were eager to demonstrate their voting power – in 1906 the Greenock Irish Nationalists boasted of their 900 voters (1/7th of the total electorate). They interpreted the Liberals' victory as a demonstration that 'the political complexion of the representation of Greenock was held by the local Nationalists in the hollow of their hands'.[62] In the Monklands, as a rule, the Nationalist ticket went to the Liberals, except for the fact that Labour seemed to appeal to some Leaguers. In 1906, the UIL instructed its members to vote for the Labour candidate, Joseph Sullivan, since the Liberal candidate, Douglas, elected in 1900, had not shown enough support for Home Rule in the Commons.[63] From an ideological perspective, the synthesis of Irish aspirations, Catholicism and Labour was driven by men like John Wheatley in Glasgow and Patrick Agnew in Airdrie. Agnew was a second-generation Irishman who did not deny his Irishness (he was one of the Foresters' local leaders) nor his Catholicity (he belonged to various parochial associations).[64] He became a member of the Labour Party through his trade union activities: in 1896, he was elected chairman of the Miners County Union.[65] When Agnew was candidate for a local election in 1909, the press stressed his ambiguous position:

> But the religious factor will certainly influence the result, and in this case, it is incalculable: for as a Catholic, Mr Agnew will probably lose many Protestant votes, while as a Socialist, he is sure to be opposed by many of his co-religionists.[66]

Beyond parliamentary elections, the Coatbridge Nationalists achieved success by having their local leader, Charles O'Neill, win a parliamentary seat in Ireland. After several unsuccessful bids, O'Neill was elected, in November 1909, MP for the South Armagh constituency. During a ceremony celebrating the doctor's success, one of the platform speakers declared:

> It is a special pleasure for us to associate ourselves with the Irishmen of London who have said with great force and point that 'your record as an Irish Nationalist has been an inspiration to the present generation of the Irishmen of Great Britain'.[67]

In addition, local leading Scottish figures were certainly proud to celebrate a local Irishman's success. A local newspaper article

DOI: 10.1057/9781137329844

claimed: 'Coatbridge, too, prides itself on your victory. From its Chief Magistrate, the Provost, downwards, your fellow-townsmen followed with eager interest every stage of the recent campaign.'[68] O'Neill's long years of living on Scottish soil (he arrived in the West of Scotland when he was 15 years old, in the mid-1860s) had even transformed his Irish character, as Father Geerty, himself an Irishman, expressed it: 'He never knew defeat and was a keen fighter, not indeed of the fiery type but more of the type of the Scotsman with his pawky but purposeful way.'[69]

Conclusion

The organization of the Irish nationalist movement in Airdrie, Coatbridge and Greenock reflected the growth of Irish nationalism as a political force across Britain from the 1870s onwards. Irish organizations were characterized by (some) electoral successes as well as dissensions and clashes amongst its members. David Fitzpatrick has reminded historians not to exaggerate Irish electoral power in Britain, as 'the "Irish Vote" in Britain was in part a bogey invented by political opponents in order to exploit anti-Irish sentiment'.[70] Yet of all three towns, Coatbridge was particularly to the fore in terms of advancing the Irish cause. Charismatic local Irish leaders were instrumental in this respect: by combining a local political career and a national(ist) calling as MP for South Armagh, Charles O'Neill gave a great impulse to the movement in his town of adoption. Although there might have been a gap between proclaimed Irish electoral strength and actual Irish mobilization, from a small-town perspective, the Irish nationalists remained a political force to be reckoned with in the West of Scotland.[71]

Notes

1   D. MacRaild (1999) *Irish Migrants in Modern Britain, 1750–1922* (Basingstoke: Palgrave Macmillan), p. 124.

2   M. Ò Catháin (2008) 'A Winnowing Spirit: Sinn Féin in Scotland, 1905–1938' in M.J. Mitchell (ed.) *New Perspectives on the Irish in Scotland* (Edinburgh : Birlinn), p. 114.

3   M. Ò Catháin (2008) 'A Winnowing Spirit', p. 115; E.W. McFarland (1998) 'A Reality and Yet Impalpable: The Fenian Panic in Mid-Victorian Scotland', *The Scottish Historical Review*, LXXVII, 204, pp. 199–223.

DOI: 10.1057/9781137329844

4   *FP*, 23 September 1865.

5   *AC*, 20 January 1866.

6   *FP*, 16 July 1864 ; 26 November 1864.

7   *AC*, 19 October 1867.

8   E. McFarland (2003) *John Ferguson 1836–1906. Irish Issues in Scottish Politics* (East Lothian : Tuckwell), p. 50. John Ferguson (1836–1906), coming from a staunch Protestant Antrim family, was the great political organiser of the Irish nationalist movement in Scotland during the late Victorian era.

9   *Airdrie Luminary*, 31 July 1847; *FP*, 9 July 1853.

10   E. McFarland (1998) 'A Reality and Yet Impalpable: The Fenian Panic in Mid-Victorian Scotland', pp. 199–223; *AC*, 19 October 1867.

11   R.F. Foster (1989) *Modern Ireland* (London: Penguin), p. 354.

12   D. MacRaild (2011) *The Irish Diaspora in Britain, 1750–1939* (Basingstoke : Palgrave Macmillan), p. 130.

13   *CE*, 2 March 1890; *CE*, 17 December 1890.

14   *GE*, 18 September 1897.

15   *GA*, 27 June 1877.

16   *GA*, 15 December 1877

17   *GA*, 19 October 1882.

18   E.W. MacFarland (2003) *John Ferguson*, pp. 220–30.

19   *CE*, 22 March 1891.

20   *GO*, 9 April 1891.

21   *GE*, 13 October 1900. Timothy Healy (1855–1931) was co-leader of the anti-Parnellite Irish National Federation in 1891, only to be expelled in 1895. He then founded the clericalist People's Rights Association in 1897 and rejoined the IPP in 1900 (see R. Foster (1989) *Modern Ireland*, p. 401).

22   I. Machin (2001) *The Rise of Democracy in Britain 1830–1918* (London: Macmillan Press), p. 74.

23   *GT*, 16 March 1895.

24   *GT*, 1 November 1887.

25   *GE*, 26 January 1901; *GE*, 6 June 1903.

26   *GT*, 2 June 1903.

27   *GE*, 30 March 1901.

28   *AC*, 21 June 1902.

29   *GT*, 13 April 1902; *GE*, 17 April 1902.

30   *GT*, 29 April 1902.

31   D. MacRaild (2011) *The Irish Diaspora*, p. 129.

32   This is argued for instance by W.M. Walker (1972) 'Irish Immigrants in Scotland: Their Priests, Politics and Parochial Life', *Historical Journal*, XV, pp. 649–67.

33   R. Foster (1989) *Modern Ireland*, p. 418.

34   *GE*, 5 October 1895.

DOI: 10.1057/9781137329844

35   GAA, GC/17/1/3: Letter from John Dougan to Vicar General Maguire, 17 December 1886.

36   *AC*, 21 August 1880.

37   *CE*, 14 October 1885.

38   *AC*, 3 July 1886.

39   *GO*, 21 November 1891.

40   D. Fitzpatrick (1989), 'The Irish in Britain, 1871–1921' in W. E. Vaughan (ed.) *A New History of Ireland VI: Ireland Under the Union 1870–1921*, (Oxford: Oxford University Press) p. 681.

41   As opposed to O'Leary's point of view: see P. O'Leary (2000) *Immigration and Integration. The Irish in Wales, 1798–1822* (Cardiff: University of Wales Press), pp. 243–44.

42   *FP*, 1 April 1852.

43   *FP*, 2 July 1853.

44   *FP*, 17 July 1852.

45   *FP*, 31 July 1852.

46   To be a registered voter, the elector had to prove 12 months' possession of his tenancy; householders had to pay their rates personally (this disenfranchised occupants of houses valued under £4 since then it was the landlord who paid the rates) ; and the receipt of poor relief in the 12 months' residence necessary would disqualify the individual. See J. McCaffrey (1970) 'The Irish Vote in Glasgow in the Later Nineteenth Century: A Preliminary Survey', *The Innes Review*, XXI, p. 33.

47   *GA*, 8 December 1877; J. Donald (1933) *Past Parliamentary Elections in Greenock* (Greenock: John Donald), p. 36; *GT*, 5 November 1885.

48   *GO*, 16 June 1888.

49   *AC*, 26 December 1874. However, as Tom Gallagher has explained, the Irish electorate was not to be overestimated as 'the Liberals had placed handicaps in the way of those least likely to be 'respectable or independent in the working-class': see T. Gallagher (1989) *Glasgow: The Uneasy Peace: Religious Tension in Modern Scotland* (Manchester: Manchester University Press), p. 69.

50   *GA*, 21 January 1878.

51   *GT*, 29 June 1892. On the Liberal Party's reluctance to support state-funded Catholic education vs. Tory support for the project, see: P. O'Leary (2000) *The Irish in Wales*, p. 262.

52   *GA*, 22 December 1877.

53   *GT*, 14 December 1886.

54   *AC*, 27 March 1880.

55   *AC*, 27 March 1880.

56   *AC*, 27 March 1880.

57   D. Fitzpatrick (1989) 'The Irish in Britain, 1871–1921', p. 682.

58   *CE*, 23 June 1886.

DOI: 10.1057/9781137329844

59 *CE*, 22 January 1887.

60 *CE*, 15 February 1899.

61 *CE*, 4 March 1899.

62 *GT*, 18 January 1906.

63 *GE*, 3 February 1906.

64 *AC*, 17 February 1900.

65 A. McDonagh (n.d.) 'Irish Immigrants and Labour Movements in Coatbridge and Airdrie, 1891–1931', B.A. Honours Dissertation, University of Strathclyde.

66 *CL*, 10 October 1909.

67 *CL*, 20 November 1909.

68 *CL*, 20 November 1909.

69 *CL*, 20 November 1909.

70 D. Fitzpatrick (1989), p. 681.

71 On the weakness of the Irish electoral threat, see P. O'Leary (2000) *The Irish in Wales*, p. 243 and 266.

DOI: 10.1057/9781137329844

7

The Impact of the First World War

Abstract: *The historian Elaine McFarland has explored Scotland's Irishmen's participation in the war effort. In line with this perspective, this chapter further pictures the impact of the Irish community's involvement and its consequences back home. Whatever the degree of Irish mobilization during the war, Scottish perception of Irish efforts was fundamentally ambivalent. From a local political perspective, this chapter also examines how the war undoubtedly contributed to an accelerated promotion of local Irish figures both on parochial and municipal boards. The Irish developed a sense of local patriotism, compatible with their Irish nationalism.*

Vaughan, Geraldine. *The 'Local' Irish in the West of Scotland, 1851–1921.* Basingstoke: Palgrave Macmillan, 2013. DOI: 10.1057/9781137329844.

DOI: 10.1057/9781137329844

The Catholic Church was active as soon as the war began: pastoral letters were read at mass to encourage young men to join the army; priests were key guests at public meetings for recruiting soldiers, and parochial societies organized soirees to celebrate their local soldiers.[1] In Greenock, an Institute for Catholic Soldiers was inaugurated in January 1915 at Fort Matilda. The Institute was funded by donations and charity sales, and it offered soldiers a chapel to pray in and a reading room with refreshments.

Irish Catholics participating in the war

After the outbreak of the war, the United Irish League insisted that the Irish join Irish units – to help recruits, the *Glasgow Examiner* advised that they should: 'Apply to a Recruiting office and state definitely – Irish company of the Irish Brigade, 16th Division'.[2] However, joining an Irish regiment was logistically uneasy and the Irish in Western Scotland ended up joining local Scottish units.[3] The roll of honour posted on Saint Patrick's church door in Coatbridge (January 1915) indicated that, amongst the 375 parishioners who had joined, only a fifth (71) had enrolled in an Irish regiment (such as the Royal Irish Rifles, Dublin Fusiliers, Inniskillings Fusiliers and Connaught Rangers).[4] The figures of Irish participation published by the Catholic press seemed to be quite high during the first months of the war: out of 15,000 Irish Catholics from Scotland in the British army in February 1915, Coatbridge had sent 1,500 soldiers, while 300 Irishmen from Airdrie and 723 Irish Greenockians had joined.[5] In early 1916, when conscription was enforced, Irish 'temporary residents' (as opposed to 'habitual residents') were exempt from joining the army. Nonetheless, defining what constituted a 'temporarily resident' Irish was problematic: for instance, Airdrie Sheriff in 1917 declared that under six month's residence, a man could not be liable for conscription.[6]

Nevertheless, Scottish perceptions of Irish efforts were twofold. On the one hand, Scotsmen considered the participation of the Irish insufficient: thus, the 1915 summer incidents at the Steamboat Quay in Greenock were regarded as proof of Irish cowardice. On 28 July 1915, the Scottish press reported on the case of James Cunnighame, a deserter from the Connaught Rangers, who tried to flee and embark on a steamer for Dublin whilst under the custody of the local police.[7] This even stoked rumours of Irishmen attempting to evade the army, and on August the

DOI: 10.1057/9781137329844

14th, Irishmen trying to embark on a steamer for Belfast at Greenock harbour were chased by a hostile Scottish mob through the town.[8] Irish Catholics protested that these Irishmen were harvesters or holidaymakers, but to no avail.[9] The stereotypical cowardly Paddy was back on stage, as illustrated by the following anecdote reported in the *Coatbridge Express*:

> A Monklands traveller says he met an Irishman newly over in a neighbouring Lanarkshire town on Saturday... 'Is it a job you're wanting?' Asked the traveller. 'Yis, sorr', said Pat. 'Come along, then and I'll get you a job where you'll have a good time and be well fed...' said the traveller, as he drew him in the direction of an army recruiting office. 'Oh', said Pat, on realising what the 'job' was, 'I don't think I'll be carin' for that kind of worrk' and he vamoosed.[10]

On the other hand, the Scottish were also ready to acknowledge Irish sacrifices in the war. This was the case when the sons of well-known local Irish figures had gone into action. In Coatbridge, the sons of councillor John Lavelle and of the late Henry Bannen were lieutenants in the *Royal Scots Fusiliers* and in the *Cameronians* in September 1914, respectively.[11] 'Patriotic Irish families' were portrayed in the local press: in April 1916, the McCartney family of Greenock had seven sons in the army (four of whom had joined *The Royal Irish Rifles*) and one daughter serving as a nurse in France.[12] Father Ryan, of Saint Mary's Greenock, was chaplain in France from 1914 onwards.[13]

Local politics during wartime – times of abeyance?

On School Boards, Catholic struggles in order to gain further privileges within the education system were intense during the First World War. With fathers and family supports gone to the warfront and with food restrictions in force, all children suffered from the war. Accordingly, Catholic members on School Boards tried to obtain support for children attending voluntary schools. In 1915, the members of the Old Monkland Board disagreed as to whether the mutual education funds should be channelled to all 'necessitous children of school age' or solely to 'children attending Board schools'.[14] When this issue first arose in late 1914, Catholic members of the board used very firm language – Father Patrick Hackett declaring: 'We want fair play and justice. We are entitled to that and we

DOI: 10.1057/9781137329844

will have it.'[15] At the Airdrie School Board, Paul McKenna, the Catholic Labour member, argued in favour of free meals for all schools.[16]

The Irish Catholic contribution to the army was also intensely disputed on School Boards: when Charles O'Neill tried to obtain free books for children whose fathers had gone into action, a census was taken of the number of Catholic and Protestant families who needed that kind of aid.[17] Out of 800 families requesting assistance, half were Catholic – this led O'Neill to declare: '[t]hat means that a bigger proportion have gone to support the army from the voluntary schools section than from the other sections of the community'.[18] Also, Catholic members endeavoured to defend voluntary school teachers: for instance, in 1917, at the Airdrie School Board, the former advocated the payment by the Board of a war bonus for teachers at Voluntary schools (as was the case for Board school teachers) on the grounds that Catholic teachers were getting lower pay than their Public school colleagues and that the Catholic community was significantly participating in the war effort.[19] Interestingly, this last argument was one of the key factors leading to the concessions to Voluntary schools in the 1918 Education (Scotland) Act. As the years went by, the complaints of the Voluntary sector representatives became more vociferous. The financial burden was considered too heavy, and Catholic schools called for transfer, but only under certain conditions. Father Hackett, one of the members of the Old Monkland School Board in 1914, declared that:

> It was only a question of time when they [Catholics] would have their rights in spite of everything because they must insist on fair play, and if they helped to collect £22,500 to educate 8,000 children, the other [Catholic] 4,000 children should get part of the money. They had the same inspectors, the same codes, the same books, the same timetable, but because they taught their children a different Catechism they were deprived of a share of the grant.[20]

The Education Act of 1918 answered their grievances, by allowing Catholic schools to become public whilst remaining under the control of the Catholic Church.[21]

A sense of local patriotism amongst the Irish had emerged before the war. Patrick Agnew, from Coatbridge, summarized these views when addressing members of the Monklands parliament for their annual dinner, in April 1914:

> After all was said and done, the patriotism that mattered in a country was love of their own town and village...Municipal administrators throughout

DOI: 10.1057/9781137329844

the country were dealing with the problems that had a direct influence on the lives of the people... Patriotism displayed towards the town in which they lived was the fundamental basis on which any country's national patriotism rested (Applause).[22]

Although all local elections were suspended during the war, Irish integration into local boards was still pending when it came to nominating new members because of the death or departure of councillors. The most striking example was that of John Lavelle, who became, in 1917, Coatbridge's sixth Provost. When Provost Davie left for America in 1916, Lavelle, as Coatbridge's longest-serving town councillor (32 years of membership), was nominated Acting Provost; he then became Provost when Davie resigned in 1917.[23] Lavelle's patriotism was certainly a fine quality in the eyes of his Scottish colleagues: by August 1915, three of his sons were in action and one of them had already died.[24] Similarly, Hugh O'Hear was elected chairman of the Old Monkland Parish Council in December 1918 (on which he had sat for 30 years) – Wilson, the Scottish member who proposed O'Hear as president, thus argued:

> There were some gentlemen present who might not, perhaps, support the motion to appoint Mr. O'Hear very readily, but he would ask them to bear in mind that this country had come through a fiery furnace during the past four years, and it was up to them to discard all prejudices and elect a Chairman who would be best suited for the position.[25]

In Greenock, things did not go as smoothly within the local boards, although there was undeniable progress. In December 1917, Neal Haughey, who had been a member of the Parish Council for 17 years, first attempted to get elected as chairman. He lost by three votes against 12.[26] However, a year later, he was close to success as his Scottish colleague, Ingram, supported him on account of his long-standing membership – but this time he lost by six votes to 20.[27]

Irish and Scottish nationalities at war?

The 1916 Easter Rising in Ireland did not have a major impact on Irish communities in the West of Scotland. The local sections of the United Irish League as well as Irish patriotic friendly societies massively condemned the insurrection. The members of the Ancient Order of Hibernians (No. 276) in Coatbridge expressed their 'utter condemnation of the attitude of

DOI: 10.1057/9781137329844

the Sinn Fein and Larkinite mob in Dublin, which is acting contrary to the expressed sentiments and sympathy of the Irish Nation so gallantly demonstrated by the Irish soldiers on every Continental battlefield'.[28]

In terms of Irish electoral strength, The Representation of the People Act (1918) changed the nature of Irish voting power. Accordingly, in July 1918, a committee was formed in Saint Mary's parish (Greenock) in order to register all potential voters.[29] The Irish Nationalists' voting instructions favoured Labour – the *Glasgow Examiner* stated in a clear manner how the Irish should vote: 'If a Labour man stands against a Tory – vote labour. If a Labour man stands against a Liberal – vote labour. If a Liberal is against a tory and there is no Labour candidate – vote liberal'.[30] In Greenock, the local politician Neal Haughey, decided to stand as candidate (he called himself a 'Labourist' although he was not affiliated to the Labour party), thus dividing the Irish vote. In actual fact, the local branch of Irish Nationalists instructed its members to vote for the English Labour candidate, Fred Shaw[31] – but the former's instructions seemed quite illogical to the local Scottish press: 'Why Mr Haughey, an Irishman and a sound Home Ruler should be passed over in favour of a Yorkshireman… we are at a loss to understand'.[32] This electoral division within the Irish Catholic community aroused anti-English feelings among Haughey's partisans:

> The Irish people in Greenock, whose husbands and sons fought nobly in this war, will expect to see their heroes reinstated in their former employment… For the past six years Greenock and other districts have been invaded by hundreds of Englishmen… Again, whilst the Scottish and the Irish of Greenock fought the Huns the majority of these Englishmen sheltered in a Government work.[33]

Such anti-Englishness could never had come to the fore before the war. Yet, although Haughey campaigned actively ('Vote for Haughey. Your Fellow Gael'; 'Vote for Haughey and make Germany pay'; 'Vote for Haughey-and-Sensible Trade Unionism' – read his electoral posters), he came last in the parliamentary fight with 9 per cent of suffrages, just behind Fred Shaw who scored 11 per cent (2,050 votes against 2,542 votes).[34]

Scottish and Irish attitudes towards foreigners during wartime throw some light on both their ways of defining 'foreignness'.[35] Of course, local Germans were the first to come under attack – and the Irish were often more hostile than their Scottish counterparts towards them. In 1916, George Mulvey, an Irish Parish Councillor in Airdrie, protested against

DOI: 10.1057/9781137329844

the leniency he felt the board was displaying towards a destitute woman whose spouse was German.[36] At a Greenock Parish Board meeting, Neil Haughey proposed in 1917 '[t]hat it be an instruction that outdoor relief be not granted during the continuance of the war to any person of German birth or ancestry'.[37] Scotsmen appeared to be more liberal regarding the definition of nationality – when the case of a Latin teacher of German origin, Miss Steinhal, was examined by the Greenock School Board in 1914, the Rev. Young insisted that: 'Her grandfather, her father and herself were British subjects... three generations of British parentage... did well'.[38]

During wartime, prominent Irish local citizens acted like their Scottish counterparts when it came to celebrating the memory of well-known local personalities. This was quite a new phenomenon – for instance, at the Greenock School Board in 1917, Father Houlihan, a Catholic priest, was the one who spoke in the name of the Board to honour the memory of the late Rev. Lennie, an Episcopalian minister who had just passed away. He declared that 'their deceased friend was esteemed and respected by every section of the community, and personally he felt his loss very much'.[39] In Coatbridge, when John Lavelle rose to address the Town Council in memory of the late Rev. Ireland, a well-known local Church of Scotland minister, he described the vicar's religious virtues: 'His boundless charity manifested for the love of his people in the ministry of God's calling... his breadth of mind and... his generous and sincere respect for the opinion of those who differed from him even on religious matters', and ended his speech with a fighting tribute 'had Mr Ireland been twenty years younger he would probably have died under shell fire administering the last rites to some local Tommy'.[40] This statement clearly indicated how participation in the war, whether real or imaginary (as in this imagined heroic death), formed a connecting thread between the Irish and the Scots.

Notes

1   *The Clydesdale Catholic Herald*, 17 March 1917; 6 October 1917.
2   E. McFarland (2003) '"How the Irish Paid Their Debt": Irish Catholics in Scotland and Voluntary Enlistment, August 1914–July 1915', *The Scottish Historical Review*, LXXXII, pp. 261–84; *GE*, 6 August 1915.
3   *GE*, 13 October 1916; E. McFarland (2003) 'How the Irish Paid Their Debt', p. 261.

DOI: 10.1057/9781137329844

4   *CE*, 13 January 1915.

5   *GE*, 19 February 1915.

6   *CE*, 5 April 1917. In the neighbouring burgh of Motherwell, local authorities considered 28 days' the longest stay for a migratory Irishman.

7   *GH*, 31 July 1915.

8   *CL*, 21 August 1915.

9   *GT*, 23 October 1915.

10   *CE*, 17 April 1918.

11   *AC*, 5 September 1914.

12   *GT*, 25 April 1916.

13   See GAA, GC/46/42: Letter from Father William Ryan to Archdiocese, 12 December 1914; *GH*, 8 June 1918.

14   *CL*, 23 January 1915.

15   *CL*, 19 December 1914.

16   *AC*, 22 August 1914.

17   *CL*, 21 November 1914.

18   *CL*, 21 November 1914.

19   *AC*, 28 April 1917.

20   *CL*, 20 June 1914.

21   J. Strong (1919) *Education (Scotland) Act, 1918. – with Annotations* (Edinburgh: Oliver and Boyd), pp. 50–7: Section 18: '(ii) all teachers appointed to the staff of any such school by the education authority shall in every case be teachers who satisfy the Department as to qualification, and are approved as regards their religious belief and character by representatives of the church or denominational body in whose interest the school has been conducted'.

22   *CL*, 11 April 1914.

23   *CE*, 26 September 1917.

24   *CE*, 26 September 1917.

25   *CL*, 14 December 1918.

26   *GT*, 11 December 1917.

27   *GT*, 6 December 1917.

28   *CE*, 3 April 1916. Sinn Fein clubs were mentioned in various sources after the year 1918: in June 1919, the *Doctor O'Dwyer* club in Coatbridge and the *Craob Padraic Pearse* club in Greenock were active. (*GO*, 24 May 1919; *GO*, 7 June 1919). For a detailed examination of the impact of the Easter Rising in the West of Scotland, see J.M. Agnew (2009) 'The Impact of Irish Nationalism on Central Scotland, 1898–1939', Ph.D. thesis, University of Glasgow.

29   *The Clydesdale Catholic Herald*, 20 July 1918.

30   *GE*, 7 December 1918.

31   *GT*, 7 December 1918.

32   *GT*, 7 December 1918.

33   *GT*, 11 December 1918.

DOI: 10.1057/9781137329844

34   *GT*, 13 December 1918; GT, 28 December 1918.
35   On the handling of Italian immigration, see: *GT*, 22 November 1916;
     AC, 10 February 1917.
36   *AC*, 13 April 1916.
37   *GT*, 30 April 1917.
38   *GT*, 4 December 1914 ; *GT*, 8 December 1914.
39   *GT*, 16 October 1914.
40   *AC*, 14 July 1917.

DOI: 10.1057/9781137329844

Conclusion

Vaughan, Geraldine. *The 'Local' Irish in the West of Scotland, 1851–1921*. Basingstoke: Palgrave Macmillan, 2013. DOI: 10.1057/9781137329844.

▶

The last return of Charles O'Neill from Coatbridge to his native land was posthumous. On 16 January 1918, his coffin 'was entrained at Sunnyside station… en route for Glasgow, and left St Enoch's at four o'clock the same afternoon for Stranraer… being taken on board the steamer at 7.30 the following morning, reaching Larne about ten o'clock en route for Glenravel [to] the family burial ground that afternoon'.[1] His funeral in Coatbridge had been an impressive one, with Irish and Scottish members of the local public bodies attending the Requiem Mass in Saint Patrick's, and the Burgh Police escorting the cortege through town.[2] The political career of that Irishman who had landed in the West of Scotland in the 1860s epitomized the intertwining of local and national scales. Not only was he a well-respected local politician in Coatbridge, but he also became a leading nationalist MP for South Armagh in 1909.[3] Yet what has to be assessed is the exceptionality of such a public calling. By the end of the First World War, there was some level of integration for the middle class Irish who participated in local public activity.

Nonetheless, public successes must not hide the fundamental fragility of the integration process. Although the official Catholic discourse on potential Irish assimilation into Scottish society became increasingly positive during the Edwardian era, there were signs indicating that the reality of Irish integration was in fact fairly precarious. The post-war era opened with the founding of an anti-Irish movement (The Scottish Protestant League) in Edinburgh by Alexander Ratcliffe in 1920 and, later on, with the publication of the infamous Report on the 'Irish race' by the General Assembly of the Church of Scotland (1923).[4] Growing displays of anti-Catholic and anti-Irish feelings in the 1920s and 1930s cast a shadow on the optimistic discourses of the prewar era. The integration process was not set in stone by the early 1920s.

The local perspective adopted in this book has shed light on the fundamental diversity and multiplicity of Irish identities in Western Scotland. From the outset, Irish immigrants were by no means a cohesive group, facing a unified Scottish urban society. What could an Irish clergyman, a mill girl, a publican and a navvy have in common apart from their (sometimes vague sense of) Irishness? The complexity of Irish forms of identity determined a variety of interactions with their host society. For instance, as regards Scottish mentalities, the Great War played a role in redefining the stereotypical Paddy – 'plastic Paddy' could appear, in turn, as the cowardly Irish when it came to Irishmen refusing to join the army,

DOI: 10.1057/9781137329844

or as the strong and invincible Paddy when Scotsmen commented upon the braveness in combat of Irish regiments.[5]

Concerning Irish Catholics, the forging of their identity in Scotland was strongly influenced by the Roman Church. However, the Church did not 'denationalize' its Irish parishioners, but operated in a complex way, aiming both at isolating and integrating Irish immigrants. The Catholic clergy thus waged a war against parishioners mixing with Protestants. The priests' arms were the setting up of separate schools and parochial societies. In that sense, priests did not encourage their Irish flock to resemble their Scottish hosts, and were tolerant towards Irish nationalism. However, alongside the objective of partly segregating its flock from Scottish society, the Church also aimed at finding its place in the fragmented Scottish religious landscape. Clerical participation on School Boards can thus be interpreted as a step towards fuller integration, which was achieved in 1918 when Catholic schools were incorporated on special terms into the Scottish national system of education. Irish nationalism also had a significant part to play in forming the Irish identity in Scotland. Its influence was, like that of the Church, also ambiguous, in that it fought for the upkeep of a separate Irishness to continue to exist for generations of migrants, and, at the same time, its local leaders' flexibility contributed to the integration of the Irish into urban society. Key nationalist leaders such as Charles O'Neill were fine examples of the successful combination of nationalist as well as local allegiances – thus showing, that combining loyalty to Ireland and local patriotism were not contradictory.

Multifaceted Irishness also included a Protestant definition of what it meant to be Irish. Effectively, the identity of Irish Protestants was influenced by geographical proximity. For instance, Orangemen would often cross the Irish Channel to celebrate the 12th of July. Their Protestantism did not always help them blend into in the urban world, since Scottish local élites proved somewhat resistant to buoyant loyal Orange demonstrations. Their Scottish hosts readily labelled them as 'Irish' rather than including them in a larger Protestant British identity. Conversely, the plasticity of national identities meant that Irishness defined Scottishness as much as Scottishness interacted with Irishness. Amongst the world of local élites, bridges were built between the Irish and the Scots through political (Liberal) affinities or professional solidarity. Such was the case, for example, with Burns celebrations when leading Irish local figures were invited to chair ceremonies organized by Burns clubs.

DOI: 10.1057/9781137329844

What does the history of Irish migrants to Scotland from 1851 to 1921 reveal with respect to the writing of the history of migrations? It gives the reader a sense that there can be *no linear history of integration*. This suggests that writing the history of the Irish must follow the same paths as migrants, with its twists and turns. Because new migrants kept landing in Scotland in the course of two centuries (although their numbers were smaller after the 1930s), issues of difference and acceptation had to be revised afresh. There is a strong need to break with the 'comfortable' tradition of story-telling emphasizing Irish successes in the new lands, as expressed in the words of the French historian Gérard Noiriel – to 'break off from the appealing writing of histories – those quiet, soothing, reassuring histories – the consensual writing specific to the rural *longue durée*'.[6]

Notes

1   *AC*, 19 January 1918.
2   *AC*, 19 January 1918.
3   *GE*, 23 December 1905.
4   M. Rosie (2008) 'Protestant Action and the Edinburgh Irish' in M.J. Mitchell (ed.) *New Perspectives on the Irish in Scotland* (Edinburgh: John Donald), pp. 145–59. See also S.J. Brown (1991) '"Outside the Covenant": The Scottish Presbyterian Churches and Irish Immigration, 1922–1938', *The Innes Review*, 42, pp. 19–45.
5   S. Campbell (2000) 'Beyond "Plastic Paddy": A Re-examination of the Second-Generation Irish in England' in D. MacRaild (ed.) *The Great Famine and Beyond* (Dublin: Irish Academic Press), pp. 266–88.
6   G. Noiriel (1988) *Le Creuset Français* (Paris: Le Seuil), p. 136.

DOI: 10.1057/9781137329844

Appendices

Appendix 1: Occupations taken from Airdrie, Coatbridge and Greenock Census samples classified according to class (I–V), 1851–71

Class I: Professional	Class II: Intermediate	Class III: Skilled	Class IV: Semi-Skilled	Class V: Unskilled
Annuitant	Bookseller	Apprentice baker	Agricultural labourer	Errand boy
Architect	Coal agent	Beamer	Bill poster	General labourer
Banker	Comedian?	Bellhanger	Blacksmith journeyman	Hawker
Chelsea Pensioner	Contractor at works	Blacksmith	Boatman	Labourer
Coal owner/master	Dealer	Bleacher	Brick maker	Pauper
General Practitioner	Draft agent	Boiler maker	Bricklayer's employee	Prostitute
Minister	Farmer	Book folder	Broker	Railway gatekeeper
Portioner	Funeral society collector	Book maker	Cabinet worker	Rural messenger
Road surveyor	Grain dealer	Bricklayer	Cabman	Tea hawker
Solicitor	Grocer	Broom maker	Carrier	Unemployed
	House proprietor	Cabinet maker	Carter	Watchman
	Insurance agent	Carpenter	Cloth darner	
	Iron Master	Clerk	Coachman	
	Manager	Clothier	Coal labourer	
	Master Carter	Coal miner	Cotton mill winder	
	Master Plumber	Collier	Dairy man/maid	
	Master X	Cook	Factory weaver	
	Pawnbroker	Cooper	Factory worker	
	Police superintendant	Cordwainer	Farm labourer	
	Rail agent	Cotton spinner	Fireman (III-V)	
	Sheriff officer	Cotton tambourer	Foundry worker	

Continued

DOI: 10.1057/9781137329844

135

Class I: Professional	Class II: Intermediate	Class III: Skilled	Class IV: Semi-Skilled	Class V: Unskilled
	Spirit dealer	Cotton weaver	Furnace keeper	
	Tea merchant	Cotton yarn dresser	Furnace labourer	
	Teacher	Cuttler	Furnaceman	
	Telegraph officer	Draper	Goods guard	
	Toll collector	Dressmaker	Groom	
	Vocalist	Engine keeper	Hay maker	
		Engineer	House painter	
		Flax dresser	Housekeeper	
		Flesher	Iron labourer	
		Gardener	Ironwork labourer	
		Gas fitter	Lathspliter	
		Hand sewer	Letter carrier	
		Handloom weaver	Machinist (III-IV)	
		Hatter	Mill worker	
		Iron Draper	Miner Coal or Iron not specified	
		Iron dresser	Oil works labourer	
		Iron maker	Pit bottomer	
		Iron moulder	Pit head worker	
		Ironstone miner	Pit labourer	
		Joiner	Quarrier	
		Mecanic fitter	Railway porter	
		Miller	Railway servant	
		Millwright	Railway surfaceman	
		Mineral check	Railway watchman	
		Mineral Dorer	Road labourer	
		Moulder	Sawyer	
		Nailer	Seamstress	
		Oil refiner	Servant	
		Painter (III-IV)	Shirt maker	
		Pirn winder	Shopkeeper	
		Pit headman	Shopman	

DOI: 10.1057/9781137329844

Pit overseer underground
Pit sinker
Plater
Power loom weaver (III/IV)
Puddler
Railway brakesman
Railway platelayer
Railway pointsman
Saddler
Salesman
Salesman
Sewer
Shanker
Shingler
Smith
Steam loom weaver
Stocking weaver
Store keeper
Strawhat maker
Tailor
Tambourer
Tanner
Taylor
Tinsmith
Umbrella maker
Waggoner
Wagon Driver
Weigher Tube Work
Whinstone dresser
Wool weaver
Wright

Signalman
Smith's hammerman
Stationary Pedlar
Stoker
Store keeper
Streamstress
Underground brusher
Washer woman
Winder
Wood cutter
Working brewer

DOI: 10.1057/9781137329844

Appendix 2:   Electoral Poster, Greenock Water Trust Elections, November 1864 [prepared from an original in the Scottish Catholic Archives, Rev. Michael Condon papers, ref: DD2/39/12]

On Tuesday we must vote in a Popish Trustee/The Clique's darling pet, CHARLIE CARBERIE!

RATE-PAYERS

TO-DAY, for the first time in the history of Greenock, we are asked to VOTE in a rank Romanist, to take part in our local Government. Can you approve of this? Will you allow […] to be inserted […] Popish leprosy in our hitherto Protestant Institutions? What are those same Popish bigots in Greenock about at this hour? They are in open revolt against their Bishop, because he will not listen to their intolerant perse-cuting spirit with which they are imbued against Scotchmen. They have the audacity to demand "That no Scotchmen be henceforth appointed to have the oversight of Irish Romanists." Is it not this trampling under their unhallowed feet the civil and religious liberty of Scotchmen, and introducing a sectarian despotism? The gentlemanly, mild and clever WILLIE GORDON is incompetent to teach our Greenock Papists, – and would-be Trustees – of the things which belong to their everlasting peace, and they long for the return of that fool-mouthed ignoramus, Father DANACHER, whose pulpit orations tended much to produce in our community riot and disorder, which required the aid of military to suppress. Now, if CARBERY and his hundreds of Greenock Romanists will not permit a Scotchman to be their priest, ought Scotchmen to allow a Papist to be a Water Trustee? SCOTCHMEN, TO THE POLL!

DOI: 10.1057/9781137329844

Select Bibliography

Primary Sources

National Archives of Scotland

AD Series (Lord Advocate's Department)
HH Series (Scottish Office Home and Health Department)
SC Series (Sheriff Courts)
FS Series (Records of the Assistant Registrar of Friendly
Societies for Scotland)

Glasgow City Archives (Mitchell Library)

CO/1 Series (Lanark County Council)
CO/2 Series (Renfrew County Council)
TD/546 Series (Papers on mining in New Monkland)
TD/729 Series (Papers of Dr. George Thomson)

Glasgow Archdiocese Archives

GC Series (General Correspondance)
WD Series (Western District)

Scottish Catholic Archives

BL Series (Blairs Letters)
DD/2 Series (Michael Condon Papers, Dunkeld Diocese)
SM Series (Mission, general 1830–78)
OL Series (Oban Letters)

North Lanarkshire Archives (Cumbernauld)

U6 Series (Monklands Photographic Collection)
U40 Series (Monklands Area Episcopal Churches)

DOI: 10.1057/9781137329844

U45 Series (Knox Collection)
UA Series (Burgh of Airdrie)
UC Series (Burgh of Coatbridge)

Airdrie Library, Local History Room

U27 Series (Monklands Archives)

Greenock Watt Library

Burgh of Greenock Series

Census Enumerators Bookscripts

Greenock (parish 564)

- 1851 East Greenock (part) E.D. 1–22 Middle Greenock
  E.D. 22–40
- 1851 Middle Greenock E.D. 41–54 West Greenock (part)
  E.D. 55–90
- 1851 West Greenock (part) E.D. 91–126 East Greenock (part)
  E.D. 127–28

New Monkland (parish 651) [Airdrie]

- 1851 E.D. 1–16
- 1851 E.D. 17–33
- 1871 New Airdrie 651/1 Landward 651/2

Old Monkland (parish 652) [Coatbridge]

- 1851 E.D. 1–8
- 1851 E.D. 9–35
- 1851 E.D. 36–51
- 1871 Western 652/1 Middle 652/2 E.D. 1–16
- 1871 Middle 652/2 E.D. 17–24 Eastern 652/3

Printed Primary Sources

Glasgow University Library

The Catholic Directory for Scotland (Glasgow: J.S. Burns),
  1845–1919.

DOI: 10.1057/9781137329844

Parliamentary Papers, Bodleian Library (Oxford)

1835 (605) XVII: Report from the Select Committee appointed to inquire into the Origin, Nature, Extent and Tendency of Orange Institutions in Great Britain and the Colonies.

1854 (382) XVI.1: Report from the Select Committee on Payment of Wages Bill and Payment of Wages (Hosiery) Bill.

1854 (396) XVII.1: Select Committee Report on Poor Removal.

1854 (1764) LIX.301: Reports and Tables on Religious Worship and Education in Scotland, 1851.

1859 Session 2 (2566) XII.449: Report of the Commissioner appointed under the Provisions of the Act 5 & 6 c.99, to inquire into the Operation of that Act and into the State of the Population in the Mining Districts.

1860 (520) XVII.1: Select Committee Report on Poor Removal.

1863 (421) LII.511: Return of Number of Paupers chargeable on the 25th day of March 1863, to each Parish in Scotland who have been born in Ireland.

1863 (518) LII.519: Copy of any Regulations, Instructions or Correspondence of the Board of Supervision in Scotland relating to Religious Instruction of the Pauper Children of Roman Catholic Parents.

1866 (459) LXI.605: Returns for each Parish in Scotland of Population, Valuation, Number of Poor on Roll, Amount of Poor Rates, and Rates per pound, 1864–65.

1868–69 (301) XI.1: Report from the Select Committee on Poor Law (Scotland).

1870 (357) XI.1: Report from the Select Committee on Poor Law (Scotland); Report from Board of Supervision on System in Scotland of boarding Pauper Children in Private Dwellings.

1873 (144) LIV.409: Return of all Cases of Disputed Parochial Settlements pending in the Court of Session and in the Sheriff Courts, and of the Time during which each has been pending in such Courts respectively.

1875 (390) LXIII.367: Return of Number of Paupers, including children, receiving relief in Scotland, who were born in Ireland.

1878–79 (282) XII.561: Select Committee Report on Operation of Laws in the United Kingdom relating to Settlement and Irremovability of Paupers, with special reference to Ireland.

DOI: 10.1057/9781137329844

1884 (218) LXII.345: Report made by the Registrar General
for Ireland, showing the Result of the Inquiries made at the
Request of the Irish Government by the Local Government Board for
England and Board of Supervision for Relief of Poor in
Scotland, as to the Diminution in the Number of Migratory
Labourers from Ireland visiting certain Districts in Great Britain, 16
June 1884.
1889 (311) X. 265: Report from the Select Committee on Emigration and
Immigration (Foreigners).
1892 (C.6795-IV) XXXIV: First Report of the Royal Commission on
Labour, 1892. Minutes of evidence, with appendices, taken before
Group A (mining, engineering, hardware, shipbuilding and cognate
trades).
1893–94 (C.7140) XLIV.709: Report to the Board of Supervision
on System in Scotland of boarding Pauper Children in Private
Dwellings.
1895 (C.7753), XXXVII: Habitual Offenders, vagrants, beggars,
inebriates and juvenile delinquents. Report from the Departmental
Committee.

Newspapers (years consulted)

The Airdrie, Coatbridge and Bathgate Advertiser (1855–1919)
The Airdrie Journal (1850)
The Airdrie and Coatbridge Luminary (1851–52)
The Clydesdale Catholic Herald (1914–18)
The Coatbridge Express (1885–1919)
The Coatbridge Leader (1899–1919)
The Glasgow Free Press (1852–68)
The Glasgow Observer (1885–1919)
The Glasgow Examiner (1899–1919)
The Greenock Advertiser (1851–84)
The Greenock Elector (1884)
The Greenock Herald and General Advertiser (1874–1918)
The Greenock Protestant (1852)
The Greenock Telegraph and Clyde Shipping Gazette (1885–1919)
The North Daily British Mail (1875–80)

DOI: 10.1057/9781137329844

Contemporary Works

Airdrie Library

Church of Saint-John the Evangelist, Coatbridge. Centenary 1843–1943. One Hundred Years of Concise History. Souvenir Booklet (Coatbridge: John Williamson Printers, 1943).

P. Drummond and J. Smith (n.d.) *Coatbridge: Three Centuries of Change* (Monklands Library Services Department).

J. Knox (1921) *Airdrie: A Historical Sketch* (Airdrie: Baird & Hamilton).

J. Lavelle (1934) *Looking Back* (Airdrie: Baird & Hamilton).

S. Lindsay (1919) *Coatbridge and the Great War*.

J. MacCarthur (1890) *New Monkland Parish: Its History, Industries and People* (Glasgow: C. L. Wright).

A. Miller (n.d.) *The Rise and Progress of Coatbridge and Surrounding Neighbourhood* (Glasgow: David Robertson).

Greenock Watt Library

J. Donald (1920) *Old Greenock Characters* (Perth: Milne, Tannahill and Methven).

J. Donald (1933) *Past Parliamentary Elections in Greenock* (Greenock: John Donald).

R. Thorne (n.d.) *A Record of the Church of Saint-John the Evangelist, Greenock 1823–1924*.

Testimonies

H. Heinrich (A. O'Day ed.) *A Survey of the Irish in England (1872)* (London: Hambledon Press, 1990).

P. McGill (1914) *Children of the Dead End* (Edinburgh: Birlinn, 2001).

P. McGill (1915) *The Rat-Pit* (Edinburgh: Birlinn, 2001).

Secondary Works

The Irish in Britain

P. Buckland and J. Belchem (eds) (1993) *The Irish in British Labour History*. (Liverpool: Institute of Irish Studies).

DOI: 10.1057/9781137329844

L. P. Curtis (1968) *Anglo-Saxons and Celts – A Study of Anti-Irish Prejudice in Victorian England* (New York: New York University Press).

G. Davies (1991) *The Irish in Britain 1815–1914* (Dublin: Gill and Macmillan).

D. Fitzpatrick (1989) 'A Peculiar Tramping People: The Irish in Britain, 1801–1870' in W.E. Vaughan (ed.) *A New History of Ireland. Vol. V: Ireland Under the Union, I, 1801–1870* (Oxford: Oxford University Press), pp. 623–60.

D. Fitzpatrick (1989) 'The Irish in Britain, 1871–1921' in W.E. Vaughan *A New History of Ireland. Vol VI: Ireland Under the Union 1870–1921* (Oxford: Oxford University Press), pp. 653–702.

M. J. Hickman (1992) 'Incorporating and Denationalizing the Irish in Britain: The Role of the Catholic Church' in P. O'Sullivan (ed.) *The Irish World Wide, vol. 5, Religion and Identity* (London: Leicester University Press), pp. 196–216.

D. MacRaild (1998) *Culture, Conflict and Migration. The Irish in Victorian Cumbria* (Liverpool: Liverpool University Press).

D. MacRaild (1999) *Irish Migrants in Modern Britain, 1750–1922* (London: Macmillan Press).

D. MacRaild (2011) *The Irish Diaspora in Britain, 1750–1939* (Basingstoke: Palgrave Macmillan).

D. MacRaild (ed.) (2000) *The Great Famine and Beyond: Irish Migrants in Britain in the Nineteenth and Twentieth Centuries* (Dublin: Irish Academic Press).

F. Neal (1988) *Sectarian Violence: The Liverpool Experience, 1819–1914 : An Aspect Of Anglo-Irish History* (Manchester: Manchester University Press).

P. O'Leary (2002) *Immigration and Integration. The Irish in Wales, 1798–1822* (Cardiff: University of Wales Press).

R. Swift and S. Gilley (eds) (1989) *The Irish in Britain, 1815–1939* (London: Pinter).

R. Swift and S. Gilley (eds) (1999) *The Irish in Victorian Britain. The Local Dimension* (Dublin: Four Courts Press).

R. Swift and S. Gilley (eds) (2010) *Irish Identities in Victorian Britain* (London: Routledge).

The Irish in Scotland

J.M. Agnew (2009) 'The Impact of Irish Nationalism on Central Scotland, 1898–1939', Ph.D. thesis, University of Glasgow.

DOI: 10.1057/9781137329844

B. Aspinwall (1982) 'The Formation of the Catholic Community in the West of Scotland', *Innes Review*, 33, pp. 44–57.

T.M. Devine (ed.) (1991) *Irish Immigrants and Scottish Society in the Nineteenth and Twentieth Centuries* (Edinburgh: John Donald).

T.M. Devine (ed.) (1996) *St Mary's Hamilton. A Social History 1846–1996* (Edinburgh: John Donald).

T.M. Devine (ed.) (2000) *Scotland's Shame?: Bigotry and Sectarianism in Modern Scotland* (Edinburgh: Mainstream).

J. Foster, M. Houston and C. Madigan (2002) 'Distinguishing Catholics and Protestants among Irish Immigrants to Clydeside: A New Approach to Immigration and Ethnicity in Victorian Britain', *Irish Studies Review*, 10/2, pp. 171–92.

J. Foster, M. Houston and C. Madigan (2010) 'Irish immigrants in Scotland's shipyards and coalfields: employment relations, sectarianism and class formation', *Historical Research*, 84, 226, pp. 657–692.

T. Gallagher (1987) *Glasgow: The Uneasy Peace: Religious Tension in Modern Scotland* (Manchester: Manchester University Press).

J.E. Handley (1947) *The Irish in Modern Scotland* (Cork: Cork University Press).

J.E. Handley (1964) *The Irish in Scotland* (Glasgow: John Burns).

J.E. Handley (1970) *The Navvy in Scotland* (Cork: Cork University Press).

R.D. Lobban (1971) 'The Irish Community in Greenock in the Nineteenth Century', *Irish Geography*, VI, pp. 270–81.

T. McBride (2006) *The Experience of Irish Migrants to Glasgow, Scotland, 1863–1891: A New Way of Being Irish* (New York: Edwin Mellen Press).

J.F. McCaffrey (1979) 'Politics and the Catholic Community since 1878' in D. McRoberts (ed.) *Modern Scottish Catholicism 1878–1978* (Glasgow: J. Burns), pp. 140–55.

J.F. McCaffrey (1983) 'Roman Catholics in Scotland in the 19th and 20th Centuries', *Records of the Scottish Church Society*, 21, pp. 278–88.

R. B. McCready (2000) 'Revising the Irish in Scotland' in A. Bielenberg (ed.) *The Irish Diaspora* (Edinburgh: Pearson Education Limited).

E. McFarland (1990) *Protestants first: Orangeism in Nineteenth Century Scotland* (Edinburgh: Edinburgh University Press).

E. McFarland (1998) 'A Reality and Yet Impalpable: The Fenian Panic in Mid-Victorian Scotland', *The Scottish Historical Review*, 204, pp. 199–223.

DOI: 10.1057/9781137329844

E. McFarland (2003) *John Ferguson 1836–1906. Irish Issues in Scottish Politics* (East Lothian: Tuckwell Press).

E. McFarland (2003) "'How the Irish Paid Their Debt': Irish Catholics in Scotland and Voluntary Enlistment August 1914–July 1915', *The Scottish Historical Review*, 214, pp. 261–84.

M.J. Mitchell (1998) *The Irish in the West of Scotland 1797–1848: Trade Unions, Strikes and Political Movements* (Edinburgh: John Donald).

M.J. Mitchell (ed.) (2008) *New Perspectives on the Irish in Scotland* (Edinburgh: John Donald).

M. O'Catháin (2007) *Irish Republicanism in Scotland, 1858–1916. Fenians in Exile* (Dublin: Irish Academic Press).

G. Walker (1995) *Intimate Strangers: Political and Cultural Interaction between Scotland and Ulster in Modern Times* (Edinburgh : John Donald).

W. Walker (1972) 'Irish Immigrants in Scotland: Their Priests, Politics and Parochial Life', *The Historical Journal*, vol. XV, pp. 649–67.

Irish Diaspora and Migration Studies

D. Akenson (1988) *Small Differences: Irish Catholics and Irish Protestants, 1815–1922: An International Perspective* (Kingston: McGill-Queen's University Press).

M. Cronin and D. Adair (2002) *The Wearing of the Green. A History of St. Patrick's Day* (London: Routledge).

E. Delaney and D. MacRaild (eds) (2007) *Irish Migration, Networks and Ethnic Identities since 1750* (London: Routledge).

D. Fitzpatrick (1995) *Oceans of Consolation: Personal Accounts of Irish Migration to Australia* (Cork: Cork University Press).

T. G. Fraser (2000) *The Irish Parading Tradition: Following the Drum (Ethnic and Intercommunity Conflict)* (Basingstoke: Palgrave Macmillan).

K.A. Miller (1985) *Emigrants and Exiles: Ireland and the Irish Exodus to North America* (NY; Oxford: Oxford University Press).

G. Noiriel (1988) *Le Creuset français. Histoire de l'immigration XIXe-XXe siècle* (Paris: Seuil).

P. O'Sullivan (ed.) (1992) *The Irish World Wide. History, Heritage, Identity. Vol. I: Patterns of Migration* (London: Leicester University Press).

P. O'Sullivan (ed.) (1992) *The Irish World Wide. History, Heritage, Identity. Vol. II: The Irish in the New Communities* (London: Leicester University Press).

P. O'Sullivan (ed.) (1994) *The Irish World Wide. History, Heritage, Identity. Vol. III: The Creative Migrant* (London: Leicester University Press).

P. O'Sullivan (ed.) (1995) *The Irish World Wide. History, Heritage, Identity. Vol. IV: Irish Women and Irish Migration* (London: Leicester University Press).

P. O'Sullivan (ed.) (1996) *The Irish World Wide: History, Heritage, Identity. Vol. V: Religion and Identity* (London: Leicester University Press).

P. O'Sullivan (ed.) (1997) *The Irish World Wide. History, Heritage, Identity. Vol. VI: The Meaning of the Famine.* (London: Leicester University Press).

Scottish and British General History

C. Brown (1997) *Religion and Society in Scotland Since 1707* (Edinburgh: Edinburgh University Press).

A.B. Campbell (1979) *The Lanarkshire Miners, A Social History of their Trade Unions, 1775–1874* (Edinburgh: John Donald).

A.B. Campbell (2000) *The Scottish Miners 1874–1939, vol. 1: Industry, Work and Community* (Aldershot: Ashgate).

H. M. Carey (2011) *God's Empire. Religion and Colonialism in the British World, c. 1801–1908* (Cambridge: Cambridge University Press).

T.M. Devine (1995) *Exploring the Scottish Past. Themes in the History of Scottish Society* (East Lothian: Tuckwell Press).

T.M. Devine (2000) *The Scottish Nation 1700–2000* (London: Penguin).

R. J. Finlay (2004) *Modern Scotland: 1914–2000* (London: Profile Books).

I. Machin (2001) *The Rise of Democracy in Britain 1830–1918* (London: MacMillan Press).

G. Walker and T. Gallagher (eds) (1990) *Sermons and Battle Hymns : Protestant Popular Culture in Modern Scotland* (Edinburgh: Edinburgh University Press).

DOI: 10.1057/9781137329844

Index

DOI: 10.1057/9781137329844

DOI: 10.1057/9781137329844

DOI: 10.1057/9781137329844

DOI: 10.1057/9781137329844

Lightning Source UK Ltd.
Milton Keynes UK
UKOW04n1638170815

257064UK00002B/10/P